MW01002964

I AM MCLOVIN

I AM MCLOVIN

HOW *SUPERBAD* BECAME THE BIGGEST COMEDY HIT OF ITS GENERATION

ANDREW BUSS

APPLAUSE
THEATRE & CINEMA BOOKS

APPLAUSE
THEATRE & CINEMA BOOKS
Bloomsbury Publishing Group, Inc.
4501 Forbes Blvd., Ste. 200
Lanham, MD 20706
ApplauseBooks.com

Distributed by NATIONAL BOOK NETWORK

Copyright © 2025 by Andrew Buss

All rights reserved. No part of this book may be reproduced in any form
or by any electronic or mechanical means, including information storage
and retrieval systems, without written permission from the publisher,
except by a reviewer who may quote passages in a review.

Library of Congress Cataloging-in-Publication Data

Names: Buss, Andrew, author.
Title: I am McLovin : how Superbad became the biggest comedy hit of its
    generation / Andrew Buss.
Description: Lanham : Applause Theatre & Cinema Books, 2025. |
    Includes bibliographical references and index.
Identifiers: LCCN 2024035027 (print) | LCCN 2024035028 (ebook) |
    ISBN 9781493079827 (paperback) | ISBN 9781493079834 (ebook)
Subjects: LCSH: Superbad (Motion picture) | Teen films--United States--
    History and criticism. | LCGFT: Film criticism.
Classification: LCC PN1997.2.S865 B87 2025 (print) | LCC
    PN1997.2.S865 (ebook) | DDC 791.43/72--dc23/eng/20241023
LC record available at https://lccn.loc.gov/2024035027
LC ebook record available at https://lccn.loc.gov/2024035028

♾™ The paper used in this publication meets the minimum requirements
of American National Standard for Information Sciences—Permanence of
Paper for Printed Library Materials, ANSI/NISO Z39.48-1992.

For my dad Ronald Buss and my grandfather, Don Buss: For bringing me to the theater to see Superbad *when I was just fourteen. What could've been an uncomfortable moviegoing experience turned out to be my most memorable movie theater experience, and one that led to this book.*

Contents

Foreword

I was sitting at a cafe in Dumbo, Brooklyn, with my girlfriend Sarah (now my wife of eighteen years), when I got a call from Judd Apatow. He said that *Superbad* was finally happening and asked me if I still wanted to do it. Four years earlier I'd directed episodes of Judd's college comedy show *Undeclared*, and one afternoon, a group of the writers, cast, and friends gathered to hear a reading of Seth Rogen and Evan Goldberg's teen comedy screenplay. Seth, Jason Segel, and Martin Starr read the lead roles. The script was terrific—authentic, raw, brilliantly funny—and in the final scene, I realized underlying it all was the fear of separating from your best friend and the waning days of a not-so-innocent form of innocence. I asked Judd to please consider me as the director if he could get it financed.

Even though the *American Pie* movies had been hits, nobody wanted this particular raunch teen comedy in 2002. But then Judd made *The 40-Year-Old Virgin* and everyone wanted to work with him. That day in Dumbo, Judd told me that Sony wanted to make *Superbad* at a "reasonable" budget of $20 million, a forty-day shoot (how I miss those days). Seth had grown too old to play the fiction-alized Seth, but Judd said he should play one of the cops and that he'd been thinking of a new SNL cast member, Bill Hader, as a good choice for the other cop. When I hung up, I told Sarah what Judd had said. The only issue for me was that I'd recently finished the script for *Adventureland*, a movie I very much wanted to make. It was also about young people, though by design a more melancholy, less overtly comedic "summer hangout" movie. Still, I worried that making *Superbad* might kill my chance of doing my own project. Sarah asked me, "Do you like the script for *Superbad*?" "Very much," I replied, "and I think I can bring something to it." She answered back quickly, "You never like anything. You have to do it."

Working with Judd and the indefatigable casting director Allison Jones, we assembled a cast beyond my expectations. I knew of Michael Cera's genius from having directed a few early episodes of *Arrested Development*, and nobody reading for the role of Seth had Jonah Hill's deer-in-the-headlights vulnerability, which counterbalanced the character's hilarious sex-obsessed bluster. Christopher Mintz-Plasse was an amazing find of Allison Jones's and made "McLovin" unforgettable by playing him like he was the coolest guy in the room. Rogen and Hader were a blast together (and it's a little disturbing how many police officers told us afterward that they're just like those guys), while Martha MacIsaac and Emma Stone made their roles so much more than they might've been—in their first auditions, they both won me over on the spot. It still amazes me that Emma hadn't been in a movie before Superbad.

Some of my personal favorites of the teen comedy genre are *Dazed and Confused, American Graffiti*, and *Fast Times at Ridgemont High*—and I thought *a lot* about those first two movies in particular because, like Superbad, they both take place in the compressed time frame of a single day. The genre may not be one that wins prestigious awards, but I believe it has a special place in movies, just as that time of life has a similar hold on our memories. Those years are painful, hilarious, and vivid.

Sometimes things come together in the best way, and on the following pages you'll see how this was one of those times. I'm forever grateful to Seth, Evan, and Judd and to every last person who worked on *Superbad*. And to my wife, who told me to not be an idiot and get on a plane to LA.

Introduction

The last high school house party. It's that moment in time where you're desperately trying to squeeze in one last epic night with your peers before going off to college and inevitably going your separate ways. There is a finality to the whole ordeal, one that hadn't been felt until then. The night is all about leaving a good lasting impression, saying goodbyes, and yes, of course, wondering how you're going to score alcohol.

More than just the final hurrah, those final days of high school represent one of the biggest shifts that happen in our lives. With turning eighteen and leaving high school comes the first sense of control that many of us will experience. Up to that point, we're at the mercy of our parents and basically anyone who is of legal voting age. With that newfound freedom comes a lot of uncertainty. There's a lot of not knowing what's going to happen as we all transition into the next phase in our lives.

Perhaps that's why *Superbad* still resonates with us so much over fifteen years since its release. Regardless of when or where you went to high school, it's impossible to watch *Superbad* and not see yourself in the film. You can't help but see your friends represented in the characters. We've all experienced the difficulty of moving away from our childhood best friend, we all know who got the first fake ID, and we all remember the embarrassing ways we tried (and miserably failed) to impress our crushes. At its core, the film rings true because of these feelings, and it's why we remember it so fondly today.

When Seth Rogen and Evan Goldberg unleashed their high school epic onto the world—complete with dick drawings, period stains on pants, guns, bar fights, and a Hawaiian organ donor named McLovin—they were riding high on the success of films like *The 40 Year-Old Virgin* and *Knocked Up*, both of which featured Rogen. These were films that, while dealing with more raunchy subject matter, were not afraid to wear their hearts on their sleeves and show the audience moments of undeniable vulnerability. Just like those Judd Apatow–directed joints before it, *Superbad* embraced that same mold and gave us something that was as surprisingly touching as it was downright filthy.

The fact that the film exists to begin with is almost a miracle in itself. While Rogen and Goldberg first thought up the film as thirteen-year-olds, it would take them over ten years to finally get the film made. Studios were nervous about whether or not they could get teenagers to come out in droves to an R-rated movie, when so few of them could—legally—get into the theater on their own. But they stuck to their guns, never doubting that what they had on their hands could work. They just waited for Hollywood to catch up with them. Thankfully, the wait was worth it.

Made for a mere $20 million, the film wound up generating more than $100 million at the box office, making it a bona fide smash hit. It raised the bar for what could be expected from a high school movie. It showed us that a teen movie didn't just *have* to be about trying to have sex—it could also have the ability to tug on your heartstrings and expose some raw nerves in the process. The days of the PG-13 high school comedies that opted to "play it safe" were officially over. There was a new generation—the millennials—that were looking to see themselves represented on the big screen. *Superbad* was what they had been waiting for.

Having characters who are as honest as *Superbad*'s goes a long way. While all other teen comedies of its day focus on the vanity of high school, *Superbad* is for the underdogs. It embraces just how awkward our teenage years can be. It manages to do this in a way that isn't cartoonish, à la *Revenge of the Nerds*. These characters have an actual depth to them seldom found in teenage comedies.

Since the movie came out on August 17, 2007, it has served as a vehicle for its stars. It features star-making performances from the likes of Jonah Hill, Michael Cera, Christopher Mintz-Plasse, Martha MacIsaac, Seth Rogen, Bill Hader, and Emma Stone. Everyone who was in *Superbad* has gone on to do big things. It goes to show not just what an eye for talent the creative team had but also the staying power of the film and its stars.

The cast of *Superbad* has among them multiple Academy Award nominations, two Academy Award wins, and a boatload of Emmy Awards. Not too bad for a film that was written by two young Canadians with no ties to the industry and a foul vocabulary chock-full of colorful expressions. If nothing else, the success of the film serves as one of the great show business stories. It doesn't matter how many times people tell you no or how unconventional your script may be. It doesn't matter how young you may be or who you know in the industry. There's bound to be someone out there who is interested in buying what you're selling. That's what happened here.

1

"We Could Write a Better Movie than This"

"**H**oly shit. *We could write a better movie than this.*"

There have been countless aspiring writers who have had this same thought after watching a sensationally awful movie. That's because bad movies can be just as inspirational as good ones. One thing most people may not want to admit is that as much as creativity can derive from being in awe, it can also be triggered by disbelief. It's the idea of, *Well, if* that *counts as being a movie, then I can do that, too.*

What they don't realize is just how much effort it takes to make even a really bad movie. A director typically doesn't set out to make a bad movie. Or if they did, they would at least never admit to doing so. Getting any movie made at all is a lot of hard work, determination, luck, and having all the stars align in a perfect formation. Yes, that includes the really horrible ones.

However, that is the thought that thirteen-year-olds Seth Rogen and Evan Goldberg had after they watched an especially bad movie. While they can't remember which one it was, they can remember that distinct feeling of disgust that set them off on the journey to make their own movie. The fact that they had no resources or connections to the industry didn't matter in that moment of impassioned criticism.

Seth Rogen and Evan Goldberg grew up in Vancouver, British Columbia. Both were heavily influenced by the films and pop culture of their youth. They also shared a mutual bond, as they were both drawn to writing pretty early on. Their first encounter happened in bar mitzvah class when they were twelve years old. Only a few months apart in age, they suddenly clicked over their common interests. As Rogen would later recall, "We became friends pretty fast. I was interested in writing and comedy, and so was he. He wrote short stories. And when you're twelve and you like writing, and you meet another kid who likes writing, it's a very easy connection. And we both liked comic books. We had a lot in common, and we started hanging out."[1]

Soon after meeting, the duo made what Rogen refers to as a "bad *Stars Wars* spoof."[2] Back then, however, their roles were reversed. Goldberg was the star of their galactic send-up while Rogen was the one behind the camera. This venture foretold, in a way, what was to come. Rogen would later point to this moment, saying that it "sparked our love of film and us spending way too much time together."

The foundation for their screenwriting partnership—and ultimately what would become *Superbad*—starts, though, with that really bad movie. There was a local video store they'd frequent that operated on a "seven" principle: you could rent seven movies for seven bucks for seven days. Rogen and Goldberg were frequent customers of this particular store, where they'd scour the shelves to land upon the worst movies they could find.

Up until that point, they were simply fans. But when the instinct kicked in to create, the preadolescent wheels were firmly set in motion. They went up to Goldberg's sister's bedroom, which is where the computer was. They weren't familiar with any screenwriting programs, such as the industry-standard software Final Draft. Instead, they opted for the readily available Microsoft Word. That's how they would write the first draft of what would eventually become *Superbad*.

At the core of the first draft—which was finished while the duo was still in their early teens—was the germ of the idea that would find its way into the finished product. From day one there was always a party, with the film centered around our heroes trying to score alcohol by any means necessary. The other blanks would be filled in over time. But the party and the alcohol were linchpins from day one.

"The first draft that we wrote—we probably finished it when we were fourteen or fifteen—it didn't have a truly discernable story versus plot, and the things that I as a writer who has been writing for a long time understands as the mechanics that great films have," said Goldberg. "What it did have was an A plot and a B plot. It had things that it was cutting between. It had setups and payoffs for jokes. It had plotlines that intertwined. It had beats that would offshoot from one another then meet back up in funny ways. As I think back to the first draft, that is actually kind of amazing both how much and how little it had."[3]

On the surface, *Superbad* has always been about that one epic party and trying to impress your high school crush. Below the surface, there's a lot more being said about that time in your life, wanting to be accepted, and not knowing what lies ahead. But these are character-development details that Rogen and Goldberg would flesh out over time. As for that initial incarnation, much of the emphasis was on what they were most interested in at that point: trying to find alcohol and fantasizing about hooking up with a member of the opposite sex. This was the world that they knew at the time, and so it would stand to reason that this is what they would feature prominently in their script.

Right around the time they were writing *Superbad* in the mid-'90s, the internet was just starting to emerge. While there was once a time when your only access to porn was browsing the adult magazines at 7-Eleven—something Rogen and Goldberg did, as Seth and

Evan also do in the script—now anyone could have access to anything they wanted. It's hard not to imagine that the access to that greater world definitely impacted the script, particularly the character of Seth. As Rogen would later say, "The internet coming out was directly linked up with me and my friends going through puberty. I literally think the day broadband came out was the day my first boner happened coincidentally. And the flood of easily accessible pornography . . . the gates were open!"[4]

Also, it should be noted that Rogen and Goldberg weren't necessarily thinking that far into the future. When you're young—and living in a place like Vancouver—Hollywood seems like a far-off place. Yes, Vancouver has always been a film- and television-heavy town. During their formative years, Vancouver would host a variety of productions, including *The X-Files*, *Happy Gilmore*, *21 Jump Street*, *Jumanji*, *First Blood*, *It* (1990), and countless others. That being said, it wasn't as if Hollywood was right next door. Instead, they viewed writing the script as just a creative endeavor. It wasn't necessarily a project they ever saw coming to fruition. It was just something fun that they could do together, almost like wish fulfillment. *What if Hollywood made a movie like this?* They just wanted to see if they could write a film.

Goldberg later said, "The straight-up truth of it is, we sat down and were like, 'Okay, let's do this thing. First, what are we going to call the characters?' That was our first issue, which is not the proper way to write a movie, but we just sat down and we literally couldn't think of names. That's how poorly we started out."[5]

Just because the characters are named after Rogen and Goldberg—and just because their experiences inspired the events of the film—doesn't mean that they were writing themselves into it from a literal standpoint. The characters aren't actually based on who they were at that point in their lives. The names Seth and Evan were merely placeholders until they thought of better ones. But they never did, and over time people seemed to like that they named the lead characters after themselves, so Seth and Evan stuck.

In the mid-'90s, raunchy R-rated teen comedies like *Porky's* and *Fast Times at Ridgemont High* were basically things of the past. Even a John Hughes film like *The Breakfast Club*—as brilliant and as influential as it may be—is tame by most R-rated movie standards. Save for a few notable exceptions—like Kevin Smith's *Clerks*—the big '90s comedies were the PG-13 movies.

As hilarious as these movies may have been and still are to this day, unfortunately there's only so much that you can really say in a PG-13 movie. Much of the humor from something like *Ace Ventura: Pet Detective* or *Billy Madison* stems from its suggestive nature, with "suggestive" being the keyword. These movies were very popular—and rightfully so. But there was a consistent, sillier thread throughout those films. Coming out of such a politically depressing era as the 1980s, the country needed to explore those type of films.

In 1999, it seemed as if there may once again be a shift, however, on the cusp of the new millennium. *American Pie* had come out, and early buzz suggested that it could be the film to reignite the long-dormant R-rated comedy genre. That movie—which stars a talented ensemble led by Jason Biggs, Seann William Scott, Tara Reid, Alyson Hannigan, and Eugene Levy—follows a group of guys who make a pact to lose their virginity. It's something that a lot of horny teenagers could relate to.

American Pie wound up being a massive success upon its release, finishing at number one at the box office during its inaugural week. While reviews were sort of split down the middle, it was a film that audiences loved, rendering it more or less "critic proof." It wound up generating a whopping $235 million globally against an $11 million budget. This was enough to spawn three direct sequels, and five straight-to-DVD spiritual sequels bearing the name *American Pie Presents*.

Upon the first film's release, Rogen initially feared that *Superbad* could—on paper, at least—be written off as being "too similar" to *American Pie* if they tried to get it made. While the two films have a significant number of differences, they still both fall into the category of "high school seniors trying to get laid," at least on the surface. *Superbad* would later distance itself even further from its predecessor. But in that moment, the concern was real.

The two films couldn't be more different when you really dig deeply into them. *American Pie* is just about guys trying to lose their virginity. You don't really get a sense for who those guys are in the film, or what losing their virginity on that particular night means to them. There are no real stakes, and for the most part, they don't necessarily care who they lose their virginities to. *Superbad* makes its stakes crystal clear, however. For Seth and Evan, this is the last chance they have to win over their high school dream girls while also being subjected to society more or less telling them "This is what you have to do. You have to be *good* at sex before you get to college."

"We like *American Pie*," Rogen later pointed out. "But I think in a lot of ways that *Superbad* was reactive to those types of movies. In those movies, there's no sense than anything other than maybe raw sexual energy is what's good and right. I think *Superbad* is more about these guys that grew up being exposed to that, not being uncomfortable with it, and how they don't ultimately subscribe to that mentality."[6]

When someone would ask them what they saw their film being like, they'd always say, "We see it like *Swingers*." Also on that list were films like *Clerks*, *Pulp Fiction*, and *Reservoir Dogs*. Not exactly what you'd expect to have influenced *Superbad*, admittedly. They were going for realism, not your standard sophomoric high school hijinks. When you really break it down, those influences make a lot of sense.

One film that people would always assume influenced the plot of *Superbad* is *American Graffiti*. There are certainly a number of parallels, such as a group of friends spending one final night together before they go their separate ways, as well as the desire to lose their virginities. In reality, Rogen and Goldberg had never even seen it—Rogen later stated that he never watched it until over a decade after *Superbad* came out. Once he finally did, he understood why people kept asking him about it.

An advantage of having two teenagers write a high school movie while they were going through it is that they could document their experiences as they were happening. As a result, there's no real sense of hindsight or perspective creeping its way into the script. It wasn't some thirty-year-old's fantasy of what he wished his own high school experience could've been, or someone misremembering certain aspects of what it was like to be a teenager. These were two boys who were basically telling the world, "This is what high school is like for us *right now*."

What high school was like is shockingly reminiscent of what you see in the film. For instance, when Evan is telling his crush, Becca, about his wild weekend, the anecdote is based on an actual wild weekend Rogen and Goldberg had where they tried to sneak into a strip club. Yes, someone really did get a period bloodstain on their pants while dancing with a girl at a party. They also really did fill a bunch of laundry detergent bottles with beer that they didn't know what to do with.

"It was inspired largely just by our desire to buy alcohol at the time," said Rogen regarding lifting scenarios from their lives. "That was very true. We liked going to house parties. We had a ton of house parties at our high school for whatever reason. And it always was a challenge to get booze. People would get fake IDs."[7]

Without any industry contacts—not to mention the fact that they were barely teenagers when they started writing the movie—they had to find a different way to get feedback. Hearing what your friends think of your ideas is informative, but you'll also want the opinions of others outside of that friend group. So they had to start thinking outside the box.

Around this same time, Rogen had been trying his hand at stand-up. He grew up watching a lot of comedy, and he was particularly inspired by Adam Sandler's comedy album *They're All Gonna Laugh at You*, which came out in 1993. Much like writing *Superbad*, Rogen tried stand-up comedy for the first time when he was just thirteen years old. His very first stand-up gig was at a lesbian bar called Lotus in Vancouver.

In one of his earliest stand-up gigs, he introduced himself by saying, "Hello, I'm Seth Rogen. And I'm a former *Playgirl* centerfold model." Despite the young age, you can clearly see in clips of his stand-up that he already had an air of comfort and stage presence. He had more confidence than most adults twice his age, and his point of view as a comedian was already sharp and fully formed.[8]

As with most stand-ups who start at such a young and impressionable age, much of his act revolved around what he knew. Therefore, he would talk about things like being Jewish, his grandparents, going to a Jewish summer camp, how the public education system is failing us, and how getting shot with an arrow is supposed to symbolize love.

He wound up honing his craft wherever he could, including at Jewish summer camp. He eventually started working all of the local nightclubs and making his presence known in the Vancouver comedy scene. This newfound career path even proved useful with gauging the viability of nascent *Superbad* jokes. He would try out bits from the script onstage and judge the audience's reaction, determining whether or not the lines were good enough for the movie.[9]

There was one story that was deemed too crazy even by *Superbad* standards. In the script, the Seth and Evan characters wind up at a party where they encounter people doing cocaine. This was based on something that actually happened to Rogen and Goldberg. However, what ended up in the movie was much tamer than what happened in real life.

A comic Rogen knew was moving away and threw a party. A lot of people from the local comedy scene were there, all in their thirties and forties. As Rogen and Goldberg were fourteen and couldn't drive, Rogen's mom had to drive them to the party and had to stay until Rogen and Goldberg decided to leave. Not only did they notice people going to the basement to do a bunch of blow, but there was also a live pig at the party. One guy decided to walk up to Rogen and start insulting his mom, telling him "Your mom's a real bitch, isn't she?" Then the pig bit Goldberg on the foot.[10]

Goldberg later recalled, "It was one of the only things where we were like, *This DID happen, but people won't buy it, so let's tone it back a little.*"[11]

Lots of the people they knew in real life get passing mentions in the script, such as Dan Remick—about whom Seth says he's had a six-pack since kindergarten. As for Steven Glansburg, Seth claims that he used to eat alone at lunch—something the real Glansburg would later go out of his way to insist was not true. Their friend Mike Snyder gets a name drop when they talk about getting fake IDs. These weren't surprises—Rogen and Goldberg were up-front with everyone about the script, and all of their friends who'd get name-drops knew in advance.

There is one person, however, who managed to get more than just a passing mention in the film. This is someone whose very name would become so synonymous with *Superbad* that if you google their real-life last name, the first thing that comes up is the film. In the script, the character Fogell—whose full name is never disclosed—is a somewhat annoying friend of Seth and Evan's. He tells the pair early on that he is going to get a fake ID, which is perfect because Seth and Evan need to find a way to get booze for a party that night. When Fogell goes to get his ID, he takes the opportunity to pick a fake name. The name he lands on is McLovin, which is a name that remained consistent in every iteration of the script. It's a name so irreverent that perhaps it could only have been dreamed up by a couple of high schoolers. They would later try to come up with a funnier name than McLovin, but they never found one. So, like using their own names in the script, it just stuck.

Despite Seth and Evan's initial reluctance, Fogell tries out the implausible fake ID at a local liquor store. Just as he's about to get the alcohol, a robber comes in and punches Fogell. The cops get involved and essentially take McLovin—a twenty-five-year old Hawaiian organ doner, according to the fake ID—under their wing for a night of chaos and mayhem: taking down a drunk at a bar, losing his virginity, and shooting guns at a cop car that's been lit on fire.

While obviously some of the more outlandish elements are exaggerations—mainly the cop stuff—there really is someone whom the character is modeled after. Fogell is based on Sammy Fogell, an actual friend of theirs. Fogell went to school with Rogen and Goldberg at Point Grey Secondary School and was present for lots of the stories that wound up in the film, including the cocaine and pig party. Sammy Fogell would later say that his onscreen depiction was "much nerdier" than he really is. However, Sammy Fogell did have a fake ID, much like his cinematic counterpart.[12]

As for the McLovin moniker, Rogen later stated, "That's something we always felt was bullshit. We didn't think anyone would actually do that. We tried to keep it pretty real, and we were aware that McLovin was pushing it a little bit. But people seem to like it. So, why not?"[13]

When you've got a script that—particularly early on—has as many raunchy things going on as *Superbad* does, one of the last people you'd probably want to share your passion project with is your mom or dad. Most kids would be mortified if their mom sat down to read something they were writing with a friend at thirteen. Surprisingly though, one of the film's earliest cheerleaders happened to be Rogen's mother. She didn't seem to mind the content at all.

In fact, she even had a suggestion about how the film could be improved. In the script, Fogell winds up having sex with his crush, Nicola. Just as they're starting, however, the cops he's befriended burst in. Because they think he's twenty-five, Fogell is about to be busted for having sex with an underage teenager—which obviously is not the case, as they are the same age. The fact that Seth Rogen's mom pitched that joke perhaps makes it even funnier.

As for the characters of the cops, they were part of the script from day one. Officers Slater and Michaels wind up having their own adventure with Fogell as part of the B story. While obviously Rogen and Goldberg—or the real-life Fogell for that matter—never befriended the cops in the way that Fogell/McLovin does, there was some real-life inspiration going on.

"They were the worst part of the original script," Rogen later said about the cop characters. "Yeah, they were always in there. The idea was that cops would always take our beer and shit when we were in high school. The joke was that, 'I bet they take our beer and go drink it in the parking lot afterwards.' Then we thought, 'What if they do? That would be funny to watch.'"[14]

In the earliest drafts of *Superbad*, there was another big difference. The characters were thirteen years old because Rogen and Goldberg were thirteen years old. Movie Seth and Evan sort of grew up with them, until they got to age seventeen. That allowed them to eventually introduce the subplot about the characters going away for college, thus bringing even more meaning to why this one particular party was so important to the duo. Once that crucial element was in play, *Superbad* found a brand-new leg to stand on.

When he was seventeen and about to enter his last year of high school, Rogen's stand-up career was taking off locally. He was working consistently, doing as many gigs as possible after school. His stand-up act allowed him to get an agent and start going on auditions. Even in the late '90s, despite the comedy boom of the '70s and '80s having wound down, stand-up comics were still being sought after by casting directors for possible parts in TV series or movies. One of the first auditions Rogen booked was for a new NBC high school series that would forever alter the direction his life would go in: *Freaks and Geeks*.

2

Along Came Apatow

Since the earliest days of his career, Judd Apatow has had a keen eye for one thing: talent. Fostering and supporting new talent has become a trademark of his. It's as if he has some sort of insight into what the next thing will be before anyone else does. This has afforded him what can only be described as an enviable track record in both film and television.

He has always been about discovery, even before becoming a sought-after producer in Hollywood. As a child, Apatow latched on to all of the rising stars of comedy. Every time these young comics would appear on *The Tonight Show* or *The Mike Douglas Show*, he would sit there glued to the TV. At a time when nobody was banging down Jerry Seinfeld's or Jay Leno's door for an interview, a high-school-aged Apatow did just that.

He would talk to various comedy club heavy hitters—who only had occasional TV appearances or sitcom stints under their belts—for his high school radio station, WKWZ. He'd do this for the likes of Garry Shandling, Howard Stern—for four minutes—John Candy, Sandra Bernhard, Harry Anderson, Martin Short, Harold Ramis, Michael O'Donoghue, and Steve Allen, who was his first interview. This was just as the stand-up comedy boom was reaching the mainstream, when more attention was about to be paid to these household names of the future.

Somehow, this kid from Long Island managed to find his way onto the ground floor of it all, with a lot of his interview subjects not expecting a sixteen-year-old with recording equipment to show up at their door. Much like Rogen and Goldberg when they started writing *Superbad*, he was not content just watching others create. He needed to create something himself, and this was his way in. If he wanted to learn how to craft a joke, who better to answer that question than actual working comics who were making a living in joke telling?

"When I was interviewing the comedians, as a kid, I was interested in the process," Apatow later said about what drew him to start interviewing comedians in the first place. "It helped me realize that they're just human beings, they worked hard, and I wanted to know how to work hard. What were the steps?"[1]

One person he didn't get to interview at the time, alas, was perhaps his biggest comedy hero of all: Steve Martin. Apatow worshipped the irreverent Martin, who was still in the arrow-through-the-head phase of his career, inarguably the biggest comedian in the universe. He was one of the first true comedy rock stars, who could sell out massive venues and arenas with his unique brand of humor. Apatow took notice.

On a trip to California to visit his grandparents, the young Apatow decided to go out of his way to meet his idol. He found out where Martin lived, and when he arrived at the address, he saw the comedian outside in the driveway. He took his chance and ran over to ask for an autograph. Martin politely declined, and told Apatow he doesn't sign autographs at his house. The young comedy hopeful instead asked Martin if he'd sign it out in the street then. Despite the impressive quick retort, Martin again refused and went inside.[2]

Apatow was so incensed that he went home and wrote Martin a scathing letter: "Dear Mr. Martin, I am your biggest fan. But I think you treat your fans like shit. I've bought all of your books and albums and gone to all of your movies. And you wouldn't live in that house if I didn't pay for everything you've ever done. And if you don't send me an apology, I will send your address to Homes of the Stars and you're going to have tour buses outside your house twenty-four hours a day."

Apatow personally put the letter in Martin's mailbox, and months later he got a signed copy of Martin's book *Cruel Shoes* in the mail. "I'm sorry," Martin wrote in the inscription, "I didn't realize I was talking to *the* Judd Apatow!" While it may have been dripping with sarcasm, it was still acknowledgment from his idol, and proof that his letter amused Martin enough to send a response. Apatow later said he felt that "if I can make him laugh enough that he would write this joke and send this joke, maybe I could do this." Also, he finally got that autograph he wanted in the first place.[3]

In Michigan another Martin diehard named Paul Feig didn't quite go to the lengths that Apatow did to share his affection with the comedian, but he was similarly obsessed with the star of *The Jerk*. Their shared love of Martin and comedy would later come in handy. Apatow and Feig crossed paths as stand-ups in Los Angeles. Feig had transferred to USC for his second year of college. Apatow, meanwhile, was enrolled in the USC screenwriting program.

"I had first met Paul in the mid-'80s, hanging around 'the Ranch,' this incredibly cheap house a bunch of comedians rented really deep in the boonies in the San Fernando Valley," Apatow later remembered. "It was all these guys who had come out to LA from the Midwest, and all they did was smoke cigarettes and watch infomercials."[4]

At a certain point Apatow hung up the mic, seven years into his stand-up career. This was because, as he always put it, he struggled to find a proper persona onstage as a comic. It was during this time that he found himself shifting behind the camera, becoming a champion of his fellow comics by working on their projects. He eventually went on to have his hands all over a wide variety of comedies to come out in the early '90s as a writer/producer, including *The Ben Stiller Show*, *The Larry Sanders Shows*, *The Cable Guy*, *The Critic*, *Celtic Pride*, and *Heavyweights*, which costarred his old comedy cohort Feig.

He was gaining a solid reputation for himself back in those days within the industry, thanks to the friendships he had forged with up-and-coming comedians such as Jim Carrey, Adam Sandler, and Roseanne Barr. But it was Garry Shandling—whom he had interviewed years earlier—who took Apatow under his wing and mentored him. Apatow wrote jokes for Shandling for the Grammys and landed a job as a writer on *The Larry Sanders Show*, where he would also later make his directorial debut. This was not something Apatow ever asked for. Instead, out of the blue, Shandling one day told Apatow, "Hey, you're directing the next episode."[5]

Feig, meanwhile, kept working as an actor, popping up on television shows like *The Facts of Life*, *It's Garry Shandling's Show*, *thirtysomething*, *Roseanne*, *Ellen*, and *Sabrina, the Teenage Witch*, where he was a semi-regular playing a teacher. In the late '90s, though, he had an idea for a television show. He wrote the pilot for the series, titled *Freaks and Geeks*, and shared it with Apatow, who immediately loved it. The script was inspired by Feig's upbringing as a teenager in Michigan in the late '70s. Unlike most high school shows coming out at that time, this one was going to be more authentic. It wasn't focused on the type of obnoxious popular kids you'd see in *Clueless*, *90210*, *Melrose Place*, or even the then-hit *Dawson's Creek*.

Instead, it was an underdog story through and through. It had you rooting for the other kids, most of whom resembled the people Feig knew growing up. It explored what it meant to be an outcast. This is something everybody who felt like they didn't fit in when they were in high school could relate to. The opening of the pilot starts out with two popular kids having a conversation on the benches by the football field. Within the first thirty seconds, the scene shifts underneath the bleachers, and there you meet the first set of protagonists, the freaks. The script was solid, and NBC greenlit the show, with Apatow on board as the executive producer.

To properly portray the undervalued, nonconventional characters, the search was on to find unique, young faces to star on the show. It wasn't going to feature your standard attractive Hollywood kids who feel like they're born ready for their close-up. They needed actors who could actually resemble someone you knew in high school. The show is notable for breaking out a variety of future stars, including Linda Cardellini, James Franco, Jason Segel, Busy Philipps, Martin Starr, John Francis Daley, and Samm Levine, as well as industry veterans like Joe Flaherty and Becky Ann Baker. For the role of Ken Miller, one of the freak characters with a sarcastic way about him, they cast a high-school-aged comedian from Vancouver named Seth Rogen.

In 1998, Rogen was sixteen and started to confront the fact that he "was probably going to fail out of high school relatively soon." Luckily, he was already three years into his stand-up career by this point, so he already had a small sense of being established within the Vancouver market. *Freaks and Geeks* was only his second audition, and was a direct result of the creatives casting the net as wide as they possibly could.[6]

"I first actually auditioned for Martin's role," Rogen recounted in an interview. "That was for the casting director, and then I was called back to read for Paul and Judd. [The monologue] I read, what's funny is that it was clearly extrapolated upon in our brains and became something that was in *Pineapple Express*. I'm talking about how I grow weed in giant underground tunnels, and I want to blow it up if it seems like anybody's going to come find my weed tunnels."[7]

Rogen's character Ken Miller is the ball-busting wiseass that every friend group has. He's the kind of guy who has a retort for just about everything. You suspect that he's probably going to fail out of high school because it didn't really mean too much to him.

If they were looking for kids that felt more genuine, they definitely got that with Rogen. He had sort of scraggly hair at the time and a distinctive voice that you could pick out of a lineup. All that was missing was the signature Seth Rogen laugh, as Ken Miller doesn't really laugh much. He has a deadpan cadence that allows him to become the perfect smartass. The stoner attributes we would eventually associate with Rogen were already fully formed here, too. Indeed, Miller—and Rogen for that matter—brought us something that we weren't used to seeing on mainstream television at that point. Everyone behind the scenes also knew they stumbled onto something special when they found Rogen.

"Everything he said made us laugh," Apatow would later recall about Rogen at that time. "The smart, sweet, grounded person we now know him to be seemed impossible back then. He seemed like a mad, troublemaking Canadian lunatic who was quiet and angry and might kill you."[8]

The show, naturally, required Rogen to move from Vancouver to Los Angeles. Because he was still a minor at seventeen, his parents Mark and Sandy made the move with him. This was definitely a big shift from where Seth was—playing comedy clubs in Vancouver—to now working on a network television show in a brand-new country. It was an entirely different sandbox for him to play in, but one that Rogen quickly adjusted to. He had also already dropped out of high school by the time he took on *Freaks and Geeks*, which at least meant that he didn't have to go to classes in between takes like the other minors did.

Freaks and Geeks premiered on September 25, 1999. Immediately, the show became a critical darling, having received universal acclaim at a time when there was no small supply of teen-driven content. Many were hailing it as one of the best new shows of the season, citing that it reminded them more of *The Wonder Years* than anything else that was currently on TV. Surrounded by a market that consisted of shows like *90210* and *Melrose Place*, something more ordinary was like a breath of fresh air. As the *Hollywood Reporter* said at the time, "The premiere, written by show creator Paul Feig, demonstrates great appreciation for the nuances of high school life. Most teen dramas divide the student body into the group that is popular and the one that isn't—the 'ins' and the 'outs.' Feig's script recognizes that, in reality, there are dozens of smaller, harder-to-define groups that merge or collide."[9]

Within the ensemble, Rogen was given lots of different opportunities to flourish as an actor, perhaps none better than an episode late in the show's run. There was a subplot that revolved around Ken Miller getting his first girlfriend, Amy, who was no slouch herself when it came to being a smartass. This new development introduced us to a softer side of both Miller and Rogen. During the episode, titled "The Little Things," Amy reveals to Miller that she was born with both male and female genitalia. The episode shows Rogen as Miller taking a dramatic turn that we hadn't seen from him before. We watch as he wrestles with what this means for his relationship, how he feels about it, and how he even briefly questions his own sexuality.

A scene like this has to be handled delicately so as not to come off as offensive. The writers were having a tough time writing that scene, so Apatow had an idea. He brought Rogen and the actress playing Amy, Jessica Campbell, into an office and taped them improvising the scene. Their improvisation informed the scene you see in the finished series. Not only did it make the scene better, but it paved the way for the model of how both Apatow and Rogen would work moving forward. Apatow later told Rogen that this was the first time he realized that the young budding star was also a good writer.[10]

This approach also allowed the scene to feel that much more real. It was the sort of performance that most young stand-up comedians don't get to give until later on in their careers. That's something that set Rogen—and the show itself—apart from the rest. As funny and ball-busting as Miller got to be throughout the series, Rogen, as the actor in these scenes, brought some legit subtlety and gravitas to the part. For someone who had never done a dramatic performance before, you can clearly see his potential. GLAAD even applauded the series and that episode in particular for how it dealt with the subject material. The improvisational approach clearly worked.

While working on *Freaks and Geeks*, it wasn't as if *Superbad* was suddenly on the back burner. If anything, the experience was beneficial because Rogen was now working within the industry. He was surrounded by richly funny and creative people who believed in telling unique stories, something that *Superbad* was a direct result of. Plus, now Rogen was physically living in the land where these things were made: Los Angeles. With Goldberg back in Vancouver, they simply shifted to a long-distance working relationship. They would spend hours on the phone talking about the film and what they hoped to do with it.[11]

Freaks and Geeks carved out a loyal fan base almost immediately. What the show may have lacked in "acceptable ratings"—as far as the network was concerned—it more than made up for in critical and fan acclaim. In the early days of the internet, fan sites dedicated to *Freaks and Geeks* started popping up. When the show's time slot was moved multiple times during the season—oftentimes a "kiss of death" in television—fans responded with multiple petitions dedicated to saving the show. They knew that there was something special going on here.

Sadly, all of the love didn't translate to the ratings. The show had an average of 6.77 million viewers, which, by today's standards, would have the network executives celebrating and touting it as the greatest thing in television. But in those days, the benchmark was much higher.[12]

There's a variety of factors that could explain why the ratings were so low. One of the biggest hurdles came from the network, which never quite knew how to market *Freaks and Geeks*. Because it didn't quite look like all of the other shows, the network wound up burying it and never really getting behind it. There wasn't much in terms of advertising, and so any good press came from word-of-mouth. The network also refused to air the show on a consistent basis. The premiere was on a Saturday night at 8 p.m., when their target audience would be out with friends. By the third episode, the show was already on a three-week hiatus, thanks to the World Series. It would then be on and off the air sporadically, with no new episodes airing during the prime month of December. So even if the audience wanted to watch it—and clearly they did—they never knew when to do so.[13]

In spite of the show being on shaky ground with the network, Rogen's outlook managed to remain noticeably positive. At the time he told a reporter, "If things just don't work out, then whatever. I'll go back to Vancouver and continue the life I had before, which wasn't that bad. Yeah, so either way, it can only be a positive thing, because I've come out ahead either way." His mother told the same reporter, however, that even if the show did end, they'd most likely stay in LA so Rogen could continue to audition for other things.[14]

One particular person at the network would beg Apatow and Feig to give the kids "a win" on the show. However, it was built into the show's DNA that they'd go out of their way *not* to highlight "wins." Instead, they were determined to depict a truer form of adolescence, one in which you didn't win all the time. You may not get to be with your dream girl, and if you finally do, she may turn out to be such a nightmare that you dump her. The show's creatives were basically drawing from their own adolescence, with no embarrassing or shameful teenage experience being off the table. It was all fair game, so long as it was authentic.

In the *Freaks and Geeks* universe, we'd see the show's protagonists ditch class, see their parents get divorced, come from broken homes, try to secure fake IDs, debate how to break things off with your clingy boyfriend, experiment with drugs, and even call out the vice president of the United States for avoiding an honest discourse with the youth. These were storylines that would keep the fans engaged, make everyone on the show proud, and make the network's head spin.

Despite all of the positive press and waves of fan support, it was not enough, unfortunately, to protect *Freaks* and *Geeks*. The show was unceremoniously pulled off the air after only eighteen episodes were filmed and only thirteen had aired. Naturally, everyone involved was crushed. They all knew that they had something special, which they all agreed on. Everyone, that is, who wasn't the network brass. Reportedly, the man who pulled the plug never really got the series because he went to private school.[15]

Apatow has been brutally honest in the years since about how responsible he felt for the show's cancellation. He believed he owed something to the young actors for having them uproot their lives—and in the case of Rogen, move to a brand-new country at seventeen—for a show that was canceled so quickly. To help soften the blow, he wound up offering them some helpful advice, which would serve them well as they would later go out and conquer Hollywood.[16] "I was encouraging everybody to write and to tailor things for themselves, because that's what I watched Jim Carrey do," says Apatow. "He had a hard time finding a job in a movie, then he found a script, *Ace Ventura: Pet Detective*, then he rewrote it with Tom Shadyac, and Sandler wrote *Billy Madison* with Tim Herlihy. They wrote their way into the movie business. So I was preaching that to everybody."[17]

Of course, Rogen was one step ahead of Apatow. He already had *Superbad* in his back pocket. Thanks to *Freaks and Geeks*, he also now had the type of industry contact he'd desperately need in order for it to see the light of day. And it wasn't just any industry contact—it was someone who had a hand in so much of the type of comedy that inspired Rogen throughout the '90s.

Rogen later recalled, "It's funny, when I met Judd and learned about all the stuff he did, I realized that's the stuff that directly influenced me. I mean, like, Adam Sandler's comedy albums were gold to me. Those were the first things that made me think, *Shit, there are things you can do with comedy I never thought you could.* And Judd helped out with those."[18]

It was around this point, once *Freaks and Geeks* was canceled, that Rogen recalled giving Apatow the script for *Superbad*. Rogen and Goldberg had just finished a version that they were proud of. They were newly eighteen, and this draft gave the Seth and Evan characters more of an emotional connection. While there would still be a lot more work to be done in that department, it was evident early on that they really had something there.

Once he read it, Apatow instantly got it. He knew it wasn't the standard script that two thirteen-year-olds would've set out to write. It felt fresher than the vast majority of films that were getting made in Hollywood at that point. Notoriously, Hollywood wasn't terribly adept at understanding how to capture the more subtle nuances of high school on film. The fact that NBC had just canceled *Freaks and Geeks* is clear evidence of this.

"Seth and Evan had an incredibly unique way of writing dialogue in the way high school people spoke, and that's what was magical about the script," Judd Apatow later stated. "I knew they were doing something no one had done before."[19]

After *Freaks and Geeks* went off the air, Rogen wound up staying in Los Angeles. If he was going to further his career, there was no better place he could be. Like all of the other young actors, he found himself treading the boards, waiting for the next big thing to come his way. He took the small role of Ricky Danforth in Richard Kelly's debut feature film, *Donnie Darko*, that starred Jake Gyllenhaal and Drew Barrymore. It's a film with a plot so complex that Rogen later said he "didn't get it, and still don't." As for the audiences at the time of its release in October 2001, they just didn't get to see it—the film was not a financial success, initially grossing a pretty dismal $517,375.[20]

A lot of this was due to the fact that it was released directly in the aftermath of 9/11 and features some unsettling scenes that deal with a part of a plane crashing into a house. Of course, the film would later go on to become a beloved cult classic, a reputation that is still going strong to this day. Though it didn't mean a whole lot at the time, it's certainly a notable film in which to make your big-screen debut.

The good news was that Apatow hadn't forgotten about Rogen. The producer was so impressed with his ad-libbing ability on *Freaks and Geeks* that he wrote him a new part on a new Fox series, *Undeclared*. The show was basically bringing the *Freaks and Geeks* gang to college—the original intention was to cast everyone from the old show on the new show. That started with Apatow writing the lead role for Rogen. The problem? The Fox network didn't think Rogen looked enough like a leading actor.

"He was already approved to be in the cast," Apatow later said, "and they literally got angry at me for suggesting it," Apatow says. "And I said, 'Let's not do the show then if we're not going to do it right.' And people threatened to sue me."[21]

To avoid a lawsuit, Apatow instead cast Jay Baruchel as the lead, Steven. Rogen once again took on a supporting part, this time playing Ron Garner. Like Ken Miller, Garner was also your typical wiseass, but in a way that was less standoffish. He was more of a calculated smartass, less of a "burnout." He was a bit more academic, cleaner cut, with glasses. In addition to playing Garner, Rogen was also brought on as a writer. At just nineteen, this made him the youngest person on the writing staff. Despite his youth, he was also one of the only people in the room who didn't have any sort of college experi-ence. Still, everyone was impressed with the volume of dialogue that Rogen could create, almost effortlessly.

The show starred a cavalcade of *Freaks and Geeks* cast members and future Apatow regulars. The show featured Baruchel, Carla Gallo, Charlie Hunnam, Monica Keena, Jason Segel, Timm Sharp, and Loudon Wainwright III, with guest stars that included Amy Poe-hler, Kevin Hart, Busy Philipps, Adam Sandler, Will Ferrell, Martin Starr, Samm Levine, Gerry Bednob, and others.

Despite being focused on the new gig, *Superbad* was never off the table as far as Rogen was concerned. It always remained a priority for him and Goldberg. During this time, Goldberg was going to uni-versity in Montreal while Rogen was working on the show. Goldberg would save up the money he made working as a lifeguard to fly to Los Angeles to work on *Superbad* and try to find ways to pitch it around town.

Like its predecessor, *Undeclared* was met with near-universal acclaim from critics and managed to carve out a pretty solid fan base. It was a show that seemed poised for success, and was again touted as being among the best of that fall's season. Sadly, another similarity that *Undeclared* shared with its high school counterpart was the fact that the network was making it clear that they didn't believe in it

Fox had initially picked up the series for a twenty-two-episode first season. About halfway through, however, they rescinded five of those episodes, bringing the total number to seventeen. That doesn't exactly suggest that the network has a ton of faith in the show. They also kept preempting it, confusing viewers as to when the show was actually going to be on. One of the producers, Kristofor Brown, said this led to family members asking him if the show had been canceled. He assured them that, at that point, it hadn't been. As the show aired, Fox just so happened to move it around a total of seven times.[22]

It didn't take long, though, for the inevitable to finally happen. By March 2002, the network canceled the show, and only fifteen of the seventeen episodes ever aired. *Undeclared* was, essentially, born out of Apatow trying to find a way to keep the *Freaks and Geeks* cast employed. But two years later, everyone was unemployed all over again.

By this point Rogen was barely twenty and already had quite a bit going for him. Few other actors can claim to have been practically plucked from the obscurity of doing comedy in Vancouver at seventeen and wind up on two critically acclaimed American TV shows. Even if the shows were short-lived, they provided Rogen with enough momentum to get things going. And the main thing that he wanted to get going was *Superbad*.

3

The Uncertain Future of *Superbad*

After *Undeclared* was—like *Freaks and Geeks* before it—unceremoniously canceled by a network that failed to "get it," Rogen could now use those shows as calling cards that could open some doors for *Superbad*. Not only was he now a working actor within the Hollywood machine, but he also had an actual writing credit under his belt. This made it all the easier to sell himself as a writer as well as an actor.

Thus, a reading was staged in 2002. Rogen was reading his namesake while Jason Segel read Evan and Martin Starr read Fogell/McLovin. Kyle Gass and David Krumholtz were reading the characters of the two cops. This marked the first official reading of the film, as well as an impromptu *Freaks and Geeks* reunion at the same time, as everyone but Gass was an alum of that show.

"I think it was probably towards the end of the last chunk of *Undeclared* that Judd told us that he was going to do a reading of Seth and Evan's script," recalls Greg Mottola, a frequent director on *Undeclared* who was there for the reading. "I heard it, and I thought *Wow. This is one of the funniest things I've ever heard.*"[1]

Mottola continues: "But it also has psychologically behaviorally astute observations about young people. They talk and act like young people, and they have feelings. They are scared. And coming to the realization that your life is going to change inexplicably when everyone heads off to college is a real thing. And them coming to terms with that or having their first insight to that. *Oh, that's actually poignant.*"[2]

The reading went well. So much so that, when it was done, Mottola walked up to Apatow and told him that—if it were to ever get made—he wanted to direct it. Despite the shared enthusiasm among those in the room, however, there remained no official plans for the film to get made. As a result, Rogen was, once again, looking for work.

During this period, Rogen did get some work from time to time. He wound up going from being a Freak to the "Creek" when he appeared on two episodes of *Dawson's Creek*. But the work wasn't consistently coming in. As a result, there was a time after *Undeclared* when he had second thoughts about his future as an actor. This was after auditioning for what he said were "a bunch of things that Seann William Scott now stars in." Despite having been on two shows that were on two major networks and going on a plethora of auditions, he found himself at a crossroads. Also, he hated auditioning.[3]

In his memoir, *Yearbook*, Rogen wrote that "auditioning is the fucking worst. A lot of the time, the room where the auditions are happening is right off the waiting room, and while you're sitting there, you can hear every other actor doing the scene before you, knowing all the while that they'll be able to hear you, too. You're often reading with a casting director or assistant, who is decidedly NOT an actor."[4]

As one can imagine, it didn't take long until Rogen found his funds quickly drying up and he desperately needed a job. By 2004, it had already been two years since *Undeclared* was canceled. During this time, a call came in to Rogen from Apatow's manager, Jimmy Miller. Sacha Baron Cohen was looking for new writers for his popular HBO show, *Da Ali G Show*. This was because, according to Miller, Cohen had a tendency to go through a lot of different writers.

Rogen was a big fan of both the series and Cohen. Cohen was a cult figure of sorts in the United States by this point. *Da Ali G Show* had aired for one successful season in the UK, and now he was bringing it to the States and doing it for HBO. Cohen's characters, including Borat, Bruno, and of course, Ali G, were already fully formed by this point. Rogen's first inclination, however, was to say no. This was because he didn't know what he could possibly add to such a brilliant show. When he told this to Goldberg, Evan convinced him that they had to at least meet with Cohen, as they both needed the money.[5]

Despite Rogen's initial reluctance, he and Goldberg—who was still at university in Montreal—took a meeting with Cohen, with Goldberg flying in specifically for it. They pitched the idea of his flamboyant character, Bruno, going to spring break in Miami. They got the job, and thus marked the first time that Rogen and Goldberg were getting paid to work together as a writing duo.

Another person who found himself at sort of an impasse during this period was Apatow. Never mind the fact that his work in television was very well received by critics and audiences. The reality was that his last two shows had failed to advance beyond a first season, and on top of that, he did another pilot called *North Hollywood*, starring Jason Segel, Kevin Hart, and Amy Poehler, that was not picked up for a series. It doesn't matter how beloved your shows may be. A single season isn't going to look good on paper to the people who cut the checks. While Apatow had worked on films in the past, the last few years were spent solely in television. So he started thinking to himself, *Maybe I should work in movies, because this television thing doesn't seem to be working the way I hoped it would.*[6]

With Apatow considering shifting his focus over to film, perhaps *Superbad* could be a possibility for his next foray. After all, Apatow was already a fan of the script, as evidenced by the reading he had staged a few years earlier. He encouraged the duo of Goldberg and Rogen to keep developing the script and add some new elements to it. He'd suggest certain areas that could be fine-tuned, and was also a big proponent of them adding more emotional and sentimental beats. As a result, he watched the story shift from just being about guys in high school going to a party to being about guys who have to face the future without having their best friend by their side every day.

At a certain point, Goldberg followed Rogen out to Los Angeles, where the young writers continued to work on *Superbad*. Oftentimes, they'd write in their underwear. This wasn't so much a creative decision as it was the direct result of their early apartments not having air-conditioning. Despite the abundance of heat in their apartment, the same couldn't be said for the amount their script was generating. They didn't really know what to do with it, as there didn't seem to be a ton of interest. They would do rewrites, pitch the film, and then, once it inevitably got rejected again, go back and do more rewrites. It became a never-ending cycle, but one that only helped improve the film.

One of the most important things that Apatow wound up helping them with is how they could end their movie. "We didn't quite realize what we'd done at first," Goldberg would later reflect. "We used to end the movie after the party, with them just walking away. And Judd was like, you didn't follow through on the emotional story. So that slowly came out."[7]

Jake Kasdan was a frequent director on *Freaks and Geeks* and *Undeclared*. When it came time to add some more sentimental components to the script, he assisted Rogen and Goldberg in going over it with a fine-tooth comb. He would then help them add more structure to it, because Rogen would be the first to admit that "we knew *nothing* about writing movies."[8]

Thanks to the various rewrites, the film started to take a different shape. What began as a story that was merely reflective of their high school experience became something much larger. Yes, they retained many elements from their teenage years, but they also gave the film a new arc. *Superbad* had found a direction for their hero's journey.

On the surface of that journey, their mission is to get alcohol for the party, earning them the respect of their fellow partygoers. More specifically, this would garner them the affection of their respective love interests. But over time, some additional layers were added. The characters became more fleshed out, and more depth was added, specifically in Seth and Evan's relationship. It would be a shame if, after following these characters for two hours and seeing their natural chemistry, it ends with them focusing all their attention on their love interests. Instead, we get to discover that it's never *really* been about the girls. It was always about them going on that quest together, and their realization of what going to different schools could potentially mean for their friendship.

In a time when a guy proudly declaring how much he loved his best friend would've been met with the toxic—and clearly offensive—expression "That's so gay," these characters wore it on their sleeves. That's why throughout the script, after it's revealed that they got accepted into different schools, everyone keeps asking them, "What're you going to do without each other next year?" Everyone knows how dependent they are on each other. While Evan may hide his codependency better than Seth, the reason he cites for rooming with Fogell—someone he merely tolerates—at college is because he doesn't want to live alone. Both Seth and Evan need each other, and it's something they've never really talked about until that fateful night.

Another thing that made the script for *Superbad* unique is that the hero's journey is ultimately fruitless. If they had been successful in their mission to get alcohol for the party—and thus close the deal with their love interests—it would've made for a very different story. Instead, by the time they get to the party, the enthused party revelers are already clearly intoxicated. Evan's interest, Becca, is so drunk that he tries to drink more to catch up with her. After he does, and just before they're about to consummate for the first time together—it's revealed that she's also a virgin—Evan gets uncomfortable. He realizes he doesn't want to take advantage of her, so he stands down. As for Seth's love interest, Jules, she doesn't even drink. All she wanted the alcohol for was her party, not herself. Seth has to come to terms with this when he realizes that he didn't need to be the booze fairy in order to win her over.

"The joke to me and Evan was always, like, in the first five minutes of the movie they could have walked up to these women and asked them on dates and the movie would have ended right there," Rogen said in an interview. "The whole movie takes place as an excuse for them not to actually talk to these girls."[9]

When you think about what's underneath the surface for these characters, it's quite sophisticated subject material for a comedy targeted at teenagers. More than that, it's something we all can relate to. This put *Superbad* in stark contrast with the other high school movies that were all about building relationships based purely on sex. While this seems to be the intention at the start of the film, the characters go through a stunning transformation after that night's events.

Rogen later stated that he viewed the movies he writes as love stories between two heterosexual men. The irony of these relationships is that they're not reflective of his relationship with Goldberg. As close as he and Goldberg are, they don't casually declare their love for each other spontaneously like Seth and Evan do in the film.[10]

Rogen would go onto say, "It's like any other movie with a man and a woman, we just want to see them tell each other how much they love each other. And I think we may have even started there and thought what other kinds of things these guys could be going through, and the whole college Dartmouth thing was what we thought would work best for the movie."[11]

As for how *Superbad* wound up getting its name, it was courtesy of David Krumholtz. Krumholtz was a child star in the '90s whose most notable role was as the elf Bernard in Tim Allen's *The Santa Clause*. Krumholtz first met Rogen when he did a cameo on *Freaks and Geeks* and later *Undeclared*. While smoking weed at the legendary Oakwoods apartments—the go-to apartments for any young child actor looking to make it in Hollywood—Krumholtz came up with the name *Superbad*. It stuck, and that became the title.[12]

With both writers in Los Angeles and a foot firmly in the door of the industry, it seemed like the perfect time to start pitching the script around. However, because it's Hollywood, the rough-around-the-edges script—while admittedly very funny—had a great deal of trouble finding traction for a number of years.[13]

"I don't remember who said it," Goldberg later said, "but it was filthy as hell and, in people's eyes, it was only for those kids—fourteen, fifteen, sixteen, seventeen-year-olds. Eighteen-year-olds wouldn't have it. To us, it was something that we hoped—even though we were kids and didn't know any better—everyone would enjoy because it's not only about *our* childhood, it's about childhood."

Similar to the issue that Apatow and Feig faced with *Freaks and Geeks*, *Superbad* was a far cry from your traditional high school movie. Most high school movies around this time were like *Clueless* or *Mean Girls*. As revered as these two properties may be, they are still PG-13 films that embrace the high school cliques, which is something that *Superbad* never did. *Superbad* isn't centered around a popularity contest. It is much more interested in character development than showing the audiences how Seth and Evan navigated the murky high school waters and found their individualism. Also, it was far filthier than *Clueless* and *Mean Girls* ever could've been. The commercial viability of both of those films probably also added to the challenge of Rogen and Goldberg trying to sell their script.

The PG-13 factor was a major sticking point for a lot of the studios the boys were pitching the film to. For instance, DreamWorks actually expressed initial interest in doing the film. Their main caveat was that the raunch dialogue would need to get significantly softened to obtain a PG-13 rating. Rogen and Goldberg were quick to say no. Had they done that, it would no longer be *Superbad* and would go against everything they set out to do. Despite needing the work, they remained firm on this point.[14]

One thing that made it so easy for the duo to stick to their guns on the issue of whether or not people would turn out for the raunchy R-rated comedy is their own experience. They could sit there and tell the heads of studios that they would personally want to see a movie like *Superbad*. As a result, it was hard for them to imagine that there weren't likeminded individuals that would do the same.

Says Apatow, "It's funny because the times have changed so much since then. But those early drafts scared people because they thought *This is too raw and graphic for a high school movie*. We couldn't get anyone to take it seriously for a while. We basically put it aside, knowing that we wanted to get it made when we were successful enough. We didn't put it on the back burner assuming it was dead forever. I think we all felt, *One day, we're gonna have enough clout to get this made*."[15]

One way to get some more clout was to bring another producer on board. For this task, they landed on Donald De Line. At the time, De Line was well established within the industry, best known for producing the films *Domestic Disturbance*, *The Italian Job*, *The Stepford Wives*, and *Without a Paddle*. So not only did they have Apatow, they now also had De Line. Two reputable producers—and they still couldn't get it made.

Suddenly, in a rather odd turn, De Line became the president of Paramount Pictures. This could've boded well for them, with their producer now in charge of greenlighting films. Alas, early on in his tenure, De Line told them point-blank, "I can't make this movie."[16]

Goldberg later said, "It should be said that he was a real champion. Like, 'This is so funny. I believe in this so much.'" But just because he believed in the film didn't mean that he was in a position to make it himself. There doesn't seem to be any hard feelings about this today, however, as Rogen would later go on to work with De Line on 2009's *Observe and Report*.[17]

The search for a studio to greenlight the film was back on. One idea that was floated was to go around the gatekeeper altogether and just make the movie themselves. As Rogen would later recall, "We had opportunities through the years to direct it ourselves, but it would have been a small independent film, and I don't really like independent films. I like big commercial movies that are meant for wide audiences. I don't see the point in making movies that only ten people will like."[18]

Clearly there wasn't any studio that was champing at the bit to make *Superbad*. Instead, one studio asked Rogen and Goldberg if they wanted to develop another idea the studio was working on instead. As they needed cash, they wound up working on a few jobs like this, including doing rewrites on a teen comedy set in ancient Rome, a project that never got made.

"There was one," Rogen later said, "where the pitch was 'teens at the beach.' I remember being like, 'What do you mean, "teens at the beach"?' And they were like, 'We just have this image. Of *teenagers*. At the *beach*.' And we were thinking, like, 'We've written a whole movie about teenagers.'"[19]

During this time, they started to shift their focus to other potential scripts, but *Superbad* was never far from their minds. In the interim, they were trying to sell other projects, such as *The Long D*—which was a college film about a long-distance relationship—or an unnamed HBO pilot that Rogen cowrote with Jason Segel and Jack Black pre–*School of Rock*. But with none of these projects taking off, Rogen and Goldberg sat back down to try writing another script.[20]

One thing you'll notice about *Superbad* is that it lacks something that would later go on to define the types of films that Rogen and Goldberg make: weed. For all the things that the characters do in the film, you never get the indication that any character is ever high, nor do you see them partaking. There is a bong in the background of the adult party that the character Francis brings them to, but that's it. For two guys who are so open about their love of pot, *Superbad* is surprisingly removed from that world.

The next script they started developing together—titled *Pineapple Express*—went above and beyond to correct that. One day, Apatow gave them the loose idea of making a weed action comedy, and they decided to run with it. The script follows Rogen as a stoner named Dale Denton and his dealer as they try to flee hit men, a drug lord, and a corrupt police officer after watching them commit a murder. The film is about as comedy- and action-packed as you can imagine, features copious amounts of weed, and even prominently showcases the "cross joint" that has gone on to become part of our pop culture.

The whole idea of working on this other script was a direct result of not being able to get *Superbad* made. Yes, it would still be a raunch film, but this was an action comedy, something that could be much more marketable if done correctly. Sadly, nobody wanted to make that movie, either. Both *Superbad* and *Pineapple Express* were—as far as the studios were concerned—DOA.

With *Superbad*'s fate still uncertain, Apatow delegated some script "punch-up" work to Rogen. Rogen had contributed—uncredited, of course—to films like *Bad Boys II* and *Kicking and Screaming*. He would also assign Rogen to write other films, like a movie for his wife Leslie Mann, but gave him and Goldberg the challenge to see if they could write it in just ten days. Again, this is another direct result of Apatow's guilt, as Rogen had uprooted his life, left high school, and moved to Los Angeles to do *Freaks and Geeks*. He continued to try to help find his young protégé work wherever he could.[21]

Apatow later said, "When *Undeclared* ended, I thought, *Well Seth is going to work like crazy. At the very least, he's going to be the funny best friend.* And then slowly we realized that no one seemed to agree with me, and that Seth was not working."[22]

Seth would recall this period of his life: "I did get jaded, I would say, at a point, somewhere in the middle of my third year of unemployment. You start to kind of blame Hollywood. I probably had a lot of tirades about how the 'Hollywood system is messed up and keeping quality projects down.' But I was just drunk and not writing, which I should've been doing at the time."[23]

As for Apatow, he was finally on the cusp of that big cinematic break he had been searching for. After spending years trying to make his mark on television, he was about to change his luck, all thanks to a fictional television anchorman hailing from San Diego named Ron Burgundy. This stroke of luck would, in turn, eventually help get *Superbad* into the right hands.

4

Breaking into Movies

By 2004, everyone was still holding out hope that maybe, someday, *Superbad* would get made, even though it still seemed like a long shot. What would bring the film closer to fruition, however, is the immediate success of another film—this one coming from an *SNL* alumnus.

In the 1990s and early 2000s Will Ferrell was white hot on *Saturday Night Live*. He became the show's utility player: you could seemingly put him into any sketch and he would find a way to get laughs. Whether he was playing a male cheerleader, attorney general Janet Reno hosting a dance party, a guy who cannot control the volume of his voice, a negligent doctor who lost a baby, Alex Trebek dealing with incompetent celebrities, or Robert Goulet singing fictional jingles, having Ferrell in your sketch was essentially a guaranteed slam dunk. When he finally left the show in May 2002, a movie career seemed imminent. While he had some film credits under his belt prior to leaving, it was clear to anyone with half a brain cell in Hollywood that Ferrell starring in films was the next big thing.

That first sure bet wound up being *Old School*. Directed by Todd Phillips, it was sort of an easy launching pad, as it was a buddy comedy with Ferrell, Luke Wilson, and Vince Vaughn about men in their thirties who start a fraternity. Needless to say, Ferrell ran off with the film, quite literally as a matter of fact. One of the film's most memorable moments comes from Ferrell's character, Frank

"The Tank" Ricard, streaking down the street at full speed. While the film received mixed critical reviews, what it managed to do was show the industry that Ferrell could not only make the transition from television to movies but also carry a film without an ensemble.

The success of *Old School* created that direct link for Ferrell's next film, *Elf*, which opened in November 2003. As crazy as it may seem today, the film that features Ferrell as a human raised by elves and traveling to New York to find his real dad also struggled to get made, going through major rewrites in the process. It went through countless rewrites and was in development hell for years before Ferrell signed on. But once it eventually happened, it made over $228 million at the box office and became an instant holiday classic.

To follow up the success of *Elf*, Ferrell turned to an idea he had for a film about a news anchor in the 1970s. The story follows self-absorbed anchorman Ron Burgundy, your stereotypical vain television news anchor, whose world gets turned upside down when—gasp—a woman enters the fray and tells him that she dreams of someday becoming an anchor. The film exposes the ridiculous misogyny of the time. Ferrell and his frequent collaborator Adam McKay toiled away at the script, and *Saturday Night Live* creator Lorne Michaels really took a liking to it. Despite that, the film was in limbo at Paramount, and nobody wanted to make it. Eventually, a deal was struck with DreamWorks to make it, with Judd Apatow producing. Finally, Apatow found himself leaving the world of TV to give films another shot.

Apatow definitely was aware of just how much the studio was banking on *Anchorman* being successful. This marked a new venture for him, and no matter how much people loved his work in TV, the fact is that his shows were never financially successful ventures. Prior to *Anchorman*'s release, Apatow lamented to Feig, "I can't keep making stuff that loses people money. They're going to figure out it's me."[1]

Luckily, he didn't have to worry about that for much longer. Backed by an ensemble cast that boasted Christina Applegate, Steve Carell, Paul Rudd, and David Koechner, *Anchorman: The Legend of Ron Burgundy* proved to be the hit film that Apatow had waited over a decade for. *Anchorman* couldn't have been received better by critics and audiences alike, and it did fairly well at the box office, making $90 million. Once it hit home video, it achieved cult classic status.

Given *Anchorman*'s success, it was only a matter of time before Apatow made his way into the director's seat. The following year, he finally got that opportunity, and he partnered with Steve Carell to create a project that could showcase their respective talents. They landed on *The 40 Year-Old Virgin*, which was picked up by Universal.

The premise is simple and, frankly, right there in the title. Carell plays Andy, a forty-year-old virgin who is content with the fact that sex is just one of those things he is bound to miss out on in life. He is happy, but his coworkers urge him to broaden his horizons, which leads him to finally meet the woman of his dreams. The story is based on an idea that Carrell had back in Chicago while he was at Second City, where he played a guy in a sketch who was trying to describe having sex when it was clear he didn't know what he was talking about.

While *Anchorman* may have blown the doors open, *40 Year-Old Virgin* was the first actual Apatow production that would have key elements that would dominate all of his future projects. There's a camp-like element to the Apatow productions, where your regular players come back each year for another summer. For *Virgin*, Carell teamed up with Paul Rudd again, as well as Catherine Keener, Romany Malco, Jane Lynch, Gerry Bednob, Elizabeth Banks, and, of course, Seth Rogen. Then you've got Apatow's wife, Leslie Mann, playing a drunk woman who vomits all over Carell. The cast was stacked with emerging stars.

As Apatow would later recall about his first time in the director's chair, "I was really afraid to direct a movie and had not really pursued it because—I don't know—I just didn't feel like I'd do a good job. And then I heard that idea and I said, 'Unfortunately, I understand what this is.'" So with that, Apatow was directing his first film, and in doing so he implemented some processes from his time in TV—like improvisation—into the film world.[2]

Once again, Apatow used the film to champion Seth Rogen as an actor. Rogen was cast as Cal, who works with Carrell's character, Andy, at an electronics store. Within the film, Rogen is given many opportunities to shine, kicking things off in his trademark deadpan style with a story about spending the weekend in Tijuana. His cameos in *Donnie Darko* and *Anchorman*—in a blink-and-you-miss-him role as a cameraman—notwithstanding, this felt like a proper film debut for his talents.

The 40 Year-Old Virgin successfully laid the foundation for what was to come. The film was a summer sleeper hit, doing everything it set out to do. Generating over $100 million at the box office, the film struck a chord critically as well. Just as he was about to start the second season of his television series, *The Office*, Steve Carell was now officially a movie star. As for Apatow, he managed to get Hollywood's attention once again.

One thing that also happened thanks to *The 40 Year-Old Virgin* is that it kicked off Rogen's film career. Initially, Rogen—who was also producing the film, as well as contributing some uncredited writing—was just supposed to be one of the guys. But because Apatow implored the actors to utilize improvisation on the film, Rogen was allowed to really stand out given how quick he was in such situations. In particular, there's one scene where he really gets to demonstrate his improvisational chops: he and Rudd exchange a barrage of insults, each preceded by "You know how I know you're gay?"

Clearly it's not a conversation you'd see today on the big screen, but such interactions were pretty prominent in 2005. The entire exchange was the result of another Apatow specialty, where he'd allow the improvisation to extend for a long time during the take. So much footage was shot that when the film went over one million feet of film stock, Kodak brought champagne to the set. You don't have to be in the industry to figure out pretty quickly that that's not common practice. Still, Rogen really manages to hold his own in the film, which didn't go unnoticed.

"While we were still shooting the movie," Rogen later recalled, "Judd (Apatow) kept telling me that the studio liked what I was doing. Then we screened it, and it got big laughs. But the real sign was when I got a call on my cell phone from Ben Stiller and Owen Wilson telling me how much they liked the movie. That's the first time I thought *Wow, things have really changed.*"[3]

Despite the success of *Virgin*, it didn't seem that things had really changed *that* much. While you would imagine it would've made things easier, *Superbad* was still not a done deal just yet. Sure, the principal players had proven track records by now. But many studios remained nervous about the material, as it made *Anchorman* and *Virgin* look so much tamer by comparison. *Superbad* still seemed to simply be part of Rogen and Goldberg's screenwriting portfolio. There had been tons of false starts—they just had to keep waiting a little bit longer.

Said Rogen, "It came so close to getting made so many times, it always seemed that it might happen. Then eventually we accepted 'We'll make this movie in fifteen years, and we'll just direct it or something.' It'll get made, so stop worrying about it.'"[4]

In 2006, Apatow teamed up again with Ferrell and McKay for a new film, *Talladega Nights: The Ballad of Ricky Bobby*. Clearly fans of working the main character's name into the subtitle, Ferrell and McKay's film follows the story of sophomoric NASCAR driver

Ricky Bobby. The comedy features an all-star ensemble that includes John C. Reilly, Sacha Baron Cohen, Michael Clarke Duncan, and Gary Cole. Unsurprisingly given the talent involved, *Talladega Nights* sped all the way to the top of the box office charts the week of its release, bringing in $47 million. In 2006, it was clear that the summer comedy blockbuster principle was still alive and well, with fans coming out in droves to see the latest offering from the man who two years earlier gave us the now-immortal line, "Go fuck yourself, San Diego."

It was *Talladega Nights* that made all the difference and finally paved the way for Seth, Evan, and McLovin. It became clear that these types of films represented some kind of movement. As a direct result, Amy Pascal, the president of Sony at the time, reportedly said something along the lines of, "I'll make every comedy that comes from these guys."[5]

"I was lucky enough in those days to make a lot of movies with Adam McKay and with Will Ferrell and with Judd," says Pascal. "It was a really great time for R-rated comedies."[6]

By 2006, the script for *Superbad* had been passed around—and passed on by—basically every studio in Hollywood that would let Seth and Evan in their front door. It had become somewhat notorious as a result, so much so that in 2006 it even wound up on the Black List, a list of all of the best unmade scripts circulating within the industry. Despite not getting made, it was still being held in high regard. But one person who hadn't yet read the script for *Superbad* was Matt Tolmach at Columbia Pictures.

As Tolmach recalls, a large part of his job was looking through scripts to find films worth making. Weekends for Tolmach were usually spent going through anything that came his way. However, as he was approaching what he considered a light weekend, he felt anxious about not having anything to read. *What am I missing?* he asked himself. To find a script to occupy his weekend, he began making calls to various friends in the industry.[7]

One such friend was Blair Kohan, an agent who represented Seth Rogen and Evan Goldberg. She asked him if he had ever read *Superbad*. When he told her he hadn't, she told him he was practically the only one and promised to send it to him. That Friday night, Tolmach sat down to read *Superbad*. It didn't take long before he was convinced of its potential.

As Tolmach recalls, "I remember closing it and thinking, *My god. That is such an emotional end to an outrageously hard-R-rated comedy*. It was so honest. I called Judd Apatow and I said, 'This is the greatest thing I've ever read.' And I called my partner Doug Belgrad and I called Amy [Pascal at Sony], and I said, 'This is a movie we have to make. Forget what you're doing. Sit down and close your door because we're making this movie.'"[8]

Tolmach was struck not just by how funny the film was but also by how authentic it felt. Still, there was a brief moment where some of the same discussions that had plagued *Superbad* in previous pitches—"Wait a minute. We can't make an R-rated comedy that's marketed to teenagers"—once again reared their ugly heads. Fortunately, Sony president Amy Pascal was not one of those naysayers.

Pascal got her start in the industry as a secretary for producer Tony Garnett. In 1986, she quickly rose through the ranks at 20th Century Fox, Columbia Pictures, Turner Pictures, and then finally Sony, where she became the cochairperson in 2006. While at Sony she developed a solid track record for herself, thanks to the studio's marketable output during her tenure, particularly the *Spider-Man* franchise. As for *Superbad*, she got it right away, being immediately drawn to the film. She understood what was at its core. After having worked with Apatow on *Talladega Nights*, she also was eager to work with him again.

Apatow has a bit of a different take on how the film got to Sony, though. According to Apatow, "One day, Amy Pascal—the head of Sony—was talking to Seth and Evan's agent at United Talent, Blair

Kohan, and she had a movie fall apart. She said 'I have to fill this slot. I need to make one more movie this year. Do you have any ideas?' And Blair said, 'What about *Superbad*?' Amy went for it, and we worked very closely with Matt Tolmach, who was the president of productions at that time."[9]

Regardless of how they got the script, the one thing that everyone remembers is that Pascal and Tolmach understood the film right away. They knew that they had something great on their hands, and they were determined to be the ones to lead the film to fruition. After so many false starts, it seemed that *Superbad* was finally getting the love it needed from the studio system.

By the time it made its way to Tolmach and Pascal, the script had already gone through endless drafts. While it still certainly had its edge—no amount of rewriting would ever take that away—the film managed to gain more of a structure and, therefore, more of a sweetness in the process.

Pascal recalls, "The thing about *Superbad* was it might have been R-rated, but it had its heart. It had its heart all over the place. And that was one of the things about those movies. The thing that I learned from Seth and Evan is that you always make movies that are essentially about friendship, and usually it's three guys where it's a three-way love triangle."[10]

In the mid-2000s, the bromance genre seemed to be gaining momentum, particularly within the Apatow camp, and it all sort of started with *Superbad*. This is something that later films from the Apatow regulars, such as *I Love You, Man*, *Step Brothers*, *21 Jump Street*, and of course *Pineapple Express*—which would eventually get made—would investigate. (There's something to be said about exploring the sweetness and love within a platonic friendship.) While at the surface the characters have a sophomoric tendency about them, there's a true and solid heart at each one's core. It's ultimately more about friendships, and sustaining those friendships, while also finding a way to balance your friends with your love interests. This subgenre gave the characters an endless depth, and *Superbad* was no exception within it.

At this point, Rogen was starting to generate some heat, not as a writer but as an actor, thanks to his scene-stealing role in *Virgin*. The attention led to his first starring role in *Knocked Up*. Apatow was once again behind the camera as writer and director—with Rogen also making contributions to the script, naturally, and Goldberg serving as a producer. In the film, Rogen plays a twentysomething stoner who accidentally gets a producer for E!—played by Katherine Heigl—pregnant. Like *Virgin*, the film centers on a very basic premise. It's not so much a situation-based concept as it is a character/performer-based vehicle.

It's characters who are keeping you invested in the story, as Rogen exudes a real everyman, Charlie Brown–esque charm on camera. While Rogen's character Ben Stone is sophomoric and refuses to grow up, it only works because he is the kind of guy you just want to grab a beer with. That warm and inviting quality always tends to come through whenever he's onscreen, which makes him a perfect leading man. He's someone you can relate to and whom you genuinely want to be around, despite his apparent shortcomings.

Practically everyone came back for another round of Apatow summer camp. You get to see some old friends as well as make some new ones. Regular repertory players were all front and center for this venture, including Leslie Mann, Paul Rudd, Jason Segel, Martin Starr, Jay Baruchel, and Jonah Hill. Hill was the newcomer to the group, having had a small part in *The 40 Year-Old Virgin* as a customer in the We Sell Your Things on eBay store who is trying to buy a pair of disco boots with goldfish in them. He's limited to less than a minute of screen time in the scene, but he was so funny—and there was a lapse in the shooting schedule that day—that Apatow decided to have him and Catherine Keener banter for what felt like hours.

More than anything else, it was probably because they just wanted to keep Hill around as long as they could.

It seemed impossible a few years earlier, but *Superbad* officially had a greenlight. This marked the first Apatow-produced film, however, where the film would be greenlit without first having actors in mind to play the parts. Finding the right talent for the roles would not be without challenge, and two in particular created an endless number of headaches for the creative team.

5

Casting from Scratch

With *Superbad* a go, it was time to get a director onboard, one who had a deep appreciation for the material. It had to be someone who could not only understand what they were doing but also find a way to elevate the story beyond your average high school comedy. After the insanely long time it took to just get somebody to agree to make the movie, it would be a real shame if it wound up in the wrong hands. Mercifully, someone who already had ties with the film was at the top of everyone's list.

Says Tolmach, "Part of the genius of assembling the movie the way they packaged it was bringing in a filmmaker. Not like 'Hey, let's get a comedy guy to do this.' Not that there's anything wrong with that, but that wasn't the idea. The idea was *We want a filmmaker who can direct performances, who can create a tone.*"[1]

Greg Mottola was a generation older than Rogen and Goldberg, having been a child of the '60s and '70s. He had made his feature directorial debut with 1996's *The Daytrippers*. The comedy-drama has a darker tone, which instantly attracted the young Canadian duo. Mottola went on to work on acclaimed television shows *Undeclared, Arrested Development*, and *The Comeback*.

To date, he had yet to direct another film. There were a few moments in which he almost found his way back into the director's chair, however—when you've directed a critically acclaimed indie film like Mottola had, studios are going to start circling around.

There were two specific instances, in fact, where Mottola almost got to make a follow-up.

First in 1999, Mottola sold Sony a script that he calls a "destination intervention." The film was to follow a group of former college friends who track down one of their number in Paris, where he is living as an out-of-control alcoholic. The film's solid cast included John Cusack, Steve Zahn, Chevy Chase, and Heather Graham. Mottola had begun location scouting when Sony decided it was a little too dark for them and killed it.[2]

Then in the early 2000s, Mottola was tapped to direct a film for Miramax called *Duplex*. The film—which eventually got made— was a black comedy about two yuppies who conspire to kill an old lady for her real estate. Harvey Weinstein felt that the film should have a happier ending like *There's Something about Mary*. Of course, that would've been a massive stretch for the material. It was always intended to be a dark comedy, and Mottola said as much. He wound up being replaced as a director by Danny DeVito, who cast Ben Stiller and Drew Barrymore as the two yuppies. Despite the talent involved, that "happier" approach didn't quite work out in *Duplex*'s favor, and it wound up being critically panned and making less than half of its budget at the box office.

Mottola found himself focusing on television directing work. *Superbad* had been on his radar, though, since he was at that first table read back in 2002. Mottola had immediately been taken with the script. After the reading, he discussed with Apatow the possibility of him directing it should it ever get made. But at that point it was looking as if no studio was ever going to pick it up— everyone was basically convinced that it was never going to happen. Then around 2004, Mottola moved from LA back to New York. Within a few months, the call from Apatow came in. He said "Remember *Superbad*? Want to direct it?" It was an immediate yes.

As Mottola recalls, "Judd said, 'It's set up at Sony. I think Bill Hader should play one of the cops. Seth will play the other cop because he's too old for Seth now. And you should come to LA and we should do this.'" In a weird twist of fate, Mottola wound up at the same studio seven years later that he almost made his *Daytrippers* follow-up for.[3]

"I've wanted to make a movie with Greg Mottola for a very long time," Apatow explained in an interview shortly before *Superbad* opened. "He directed some episodes of *Undeclared,* and I loved his film *The Daytrippers*—it seemed like the perfect combination. Because we wanted this movie to be aggressively funny and dirty and foul-mouthed, but it's also at its core supposed to be a sweet movie about two guys who are panicking because high school has ended and they're not going to go to the same college. And I thought that Greg could really deepen the story and take it more seriously while still allowing it to be hopefully incredibly funny."[4]

Another person who had first heard about *Superbad* early on that came aboard was producer Shauna Robertson. Her first exposure to the film was when she met Rogen and Goldberg years earlier and tried to help them get it made. Robertson had been working in the industry since the early '90s, when she started out as an assistant to comedian-turned-filmmaker Mike Binder. Apatow had produced Binder's second film, *Crossing the Bridge.* Robertson wound up becoming a producer not long after that, starting with *Mystery, Alaska* in 1999. This was followed by *Meet the Parents, Elf,* and *Anchorman.* Not unlike Apatow, she had a track record by this point was seemingly unheard of: the last three films she had produced were all critical and commercial successes.

"The characters were true to who they really were, because they really are Seth and Evan," Roberston said about the script for *Super-bad.* "I knew Seth and Evan pretty darn well, so when I read it, I was like, *Wow. This is like going through their high school experience,* which is very similar to mine. I grew up in Canada also and had crazy stories about fake IDs. I just felt that it was a universal story, and we crossed our fingers that it would be everyone else's universal story as well."[5]

From the time the boys started writing the script until the earliest table reads, Rogen was always going to play Seth. That's not quite why they named the character Seth, but it was sort of the expectation. After all, Rogen had already proven what he could do as an actor, so it seemed natural. However, things ultimately weren't meant to be.

The road to making the film was obviously a long one. It might not have seemed like that to the average moviegoer because *Superbad* came out only a few months after Rogen's starring vehicle *Knocked Up*. By that point, he was starting to pick up steam within the industry. But that's ignoring the fact that Rogen was first introduced to the public nearly eight years earlier on *Freaks and Geeks*. That he was barely in his mid-twenties by the time it finally came out only furthered this assumption that he was an overnight success.

The reality, of course, is that there was a ten-year trajectory from the first draft until cameras even started to roll. During that time, it became apparent to everyone involved—including Rogen himself—that he no longer looked the part of a high school student. If you saw him wandering through the halls of a high school, you'd instantly think he was a faculty member of some sort.

"Going back to high school, Seth and I were the oldest looking," Goldberg later recalled. "We would wear our bar mitzvah suits and not shave for a week, and that's how we actually bought liquor. Seth was always one of the older-looking kids."[6]

One of the things that made *Freaks and Geeks* so special was just how realistic it all seemed. It matched your memories of being in high school. Part of this is because, with a few notable exceptions, the majority of the actors were actual teenagers during production. That is in stark contrast to the traditional Hollywood model of casting adults, because production wouldn't have to adhere to child labor laws, and the adults could work longer hours. Like anything else in show business, it always comes back to the business side of things.

The decision to have Rogen not play Seth came while they were still trying to pitch the script around town. So throughout the final few years of trying to get it made, Rogen was always going to play the cop. Once Apatow's involvement allowed the film to get green-lit, however, they were finally able to start thinking about who was going to play Seth. To cast the film, they turned to the legendary casting director Allison Jones. It was Jones, after all, who first discovered Seth Rogen back in 1999.

Jones got her start in the TV world, casting for *Day by Day*, *Family Ties*, *Boy Meets World*, *The Fresh Prince of Bel-Air*, and a slew of made-for-TV movies, most of which were for the Disney Channel. In 1999, Apatow brought her on to cast *Freaks and Geeks*. Her work on the show even won her an Emmy, which is no small feat considering that the show had already been canceled for six months by the time she got her trophy. She later went on to work on *Undeclared* before Apatow brought her into the film world for *The 40 Year-Old Virgin*, which led to *Talladega Nights*, *Borat*, *Knocked Up*, and *Hot Rod*, not including the countless films she's worked on since. By 2006 she was a pro at leaving her indelible mark on the world of comedy, which made her the perfect choice to cast *Superbad*.

If you have a project to cast, Jones is the best you can possibly get. As a result, she is highly regarded as a legend within the industry, and is responsible for discovering so many talented, unknown actors and attaching them to the projects that they would forever become identified with. That's why Apatow has brought her on to virtually every project he's ever done, starting with *Freaks and Geeks* and continuing to this day.

If you thought the hard part of making *Superbad* was getting a studio to put up the money for it, you'd be sorely mistaken. Just as the road to getting the film greenlit was challenging, the same could be said for the casting process, which Goldberg has referred to as "the longest, most time-consuming thing I have ever done in my entire life."[7]

To cast the film, Rogen, Goldberg, Mottola, and Robertson met with every young actor in the industry they could think of. Again, this was the first Apatow production that wasn't precast when it got the green light. They had to start with a clean slate. As a result, the process was as tedious as it was long.

A revolving door of young actors in Hollywood were considered for the Seth and Evan roles. Michael Cera's name came up pretty early on in the process. Greg Mottola had directed a few episodes of *Arrested Development*, so he was familiar with him through the series. Rogen and Goldberg hadn't yet seen *Arrested Development* by the time they were casting the role. It was actually Jay Baruchel—who wasn't even involved in *Superbad* but whom Rogen remained close with after *Undeclared*—who was pushing for them to cast Cera as Evan. Before Cera even got to read the script, his mom had gone through it first and suggested that her son give it a go.

"I remember that I went in several times, reading with several different actors who were auditioning for the role of Seth, and just feeling a continual hopefulness that I was in the running," Cera later recalled. "It definitely felt positive that they kept bringing me back."[8]

From the beginning of his taped reading opposite Rogen—who was standing in for the Seth character—it was clear that nobody else could play this role. Dressed in a striped sweater, no older than seventeen at this point, Cera is notably completely off script and at ease. His effortless charm was instantly apparent, even when he's getting pissed off. He managed to hold his own against Rogen, which is no small feat for any actor, particularly when having to deliver comedic lines like "If you told me we were going to burn our dicks off and I didn't do it, that's not bailing. That's self-preservation." In his audition, he completely unloads on Seth, telling him, "Because of you, I'm going to college a friendless virgin!" There was so much passion in his performance—and no hint of any intimidation in his voice—that they could've started shooting the movie that very second. He was that solid.[9]

On paper, the role of Evan can be challenging. So much of Evan's character relies on his inherent awkwardness, which by and large comes out of the acting choices Michael Cera makes for him. Cera embraces the inner awkwardness that we all felt as teenagers and manages to bring it to the forefront. Evan couldn't be played as the second-banana type. Even though the Seth character steals away a lot of the focus in their scenes together, it's important for Evan to hold his own. They needed someone who not only was comfortable with the part but could also make it believable that they would put up with Seth's over-the-top nature for as long as they had.

In this regard, Cera is clearly a natural. Even in just his taped reading, you can sense the loyalty of his character. You get the sense that he is the kind of person who would keep Seth around, even though the rest of the school may have been quick to write him off. Within his two-minute audition, Cera got to the depth of who Evan is.

That Michael Cera would have such a natural presence in an audition should serve as no surprise. Born and raised in Ontario, Cera got his start as a young child actor in a Tim Hortons commercial, for which he wasn't paid. Having started so young, he definitely got to see from an early age just how tough auditioning is, which would mean the process was old hat by the time he got into the room with Rogen.

One of the earliest auditions he went on, as a matter of fact, was for the role of Cole Sear in the M. Night Shyamalan film *The Sixth Sense*. The scene that Cera was given to read ended with Sear tearfully telling Bruce Willis's character, "Some magic's real." However, as he wasn't given the emotional context of the scene, Cera cheerfully delivered the line more as an exclamation. The role went to Haley Joel Osment.[10]

After that, he wound up getting a role on the Canadian series *I Was a Sixth Grade Alien*. He did a wide variety of other television work, including the TV film *Switching Goals* opposite the Olsen twins. His first prominent film role was playing a young Chuck Barris in George Clooney's *Confessions of a Dangerous Mind*.

But it was *Arrested Development* that brought him widespread attention. Whenever there's a list of television shows that were canceled too soon, *Freaks and Geeks* is always in good company alongside *Arrested Development*. Both shows have stellar casts, with *Arrested Development* featuring Jason Bateman, Will Arnett, Portia de Rossi, Jeffrey Tambor, David Cross, Tony Hale, Jessica Walter, and Cera, who played Bateman's son, George Michael.

Like Evan, George Michael also has an innocent—if not awkward—charm to him. Like *Freaks and Geeks*, *Arrested Development* also developed a really loyal fanbase, and it, too, was at the mercy of a network—Fox, again—that didn't know what it had. By the time *Superbad* came along, *Arrested Development* had just been canceled after only three seasons. Despite Cera's success on television, though, *Superbad* was going to mark his first leading role in a film. With Cera securing the role of Evan, the pressure on the filmmakers gained an additional layer—they now had to find someone just as good to play Seth.

As they were searching for their Seth, part of the process included reads with Cera. What followed was a never-ending lineup of hopeful actors who couldn't quite capture what they were looking for. As Apatow points out, this was because there didn't seem to be anybody who was coming in to read that was as funny as Michael Cera. They got close to hiring a few different actors, but then as soon as one would read with Cera, it was immediately apparent that it wasn't going to work. The chemistry was just never there.[11]

Rogen would later recount, "He had to read with everybody. There was a point in Michael Cera's life where his full-time job was coming into a casting office and reading with actors who were just screaming at him all day."[12]

No matter how many people they had to go through to find Seth, they could all agree on a single thing: they were dead set against Jonah Hill playing the role.

Hill was born in Los Angeles to a costume designer and the tour accountant for Guns N' Roses. Growing up there, he spent a lot of his time skateboarding, something he would feature prominently years later in his directorial debut, *Mid90s*. After college, Hill found himself in New York, where he would write plays and perform them in an East Village bar called Black and White. His first film role came about as a result of Hill's friendship with Rebecca and Jake Hoffman, who introduced them to their dad, Dustin. Hoffman, in turn, asked Hill to audition for his next project, *I Heart Huckabees*, directed by David O. Russell, in which Hill was cast in a very small role. One minute, Hill was working a job making boxes; the next, he managed to land his first part in a star-studded film.

Huckabees allowed Hill to get himself a manager, whom he told the one person he wanted to meet with was Judd Apatow, who at the time was fresh off producing *Anchorman*. The meeting happened, and Hill became a player in their world starting with *The 40 Year-Old Virgin*. Prior to his audition for that part, Hill was at a screening of Wes Anderson's *The Life Aquatic with Steve Zissou*. Sitting in front of him was Rogen, and the two quickly hit it off. Given their off-camera friendship, Hill was given a part as one of Rogen's on-camera friends in *Knocked Up*.[13]

As soon as he read *Superbad*, though, Hill fell in love with the script. During a table read, he wound up acting as a utility player, reading the part of Francis—who brings Seth and Evan to the adult party—as well as various other parts. But from the first time he read the script, he was especially drawn to the character of Seth. He knew that he was perfect for the part. It was difficult to convince everyone else involved—including Rogen, Goldberg, Apatow, and Mottola—that it should be him. The conversation always came back to the same thing: Hill was too old.

"We all knew Jonah and knew Jonah was great," Mottola says. "But I got it in my head that we had to be careful to cast people who felt young. Jonah has a very youthful [look], but I was like 'Let's just read people who are closer to the actual age,' because Jonah was like in his early twenties."[14]

"I was told that I was too old," Hill later said in an interview. "I knew Judd, and Evan, and Seth so well. Seth and Evan are like a year apart. They looked at me as if I were the same age as them. So why would I play a high school student? Especially since I'd just played one of Seth's friends in *Knocked Up*. So, essentially, I really wanted to play it. It was the funniest script I had ever read. But I was just considered too old to play it."[15]

The last thing they wanted was for the film to run into the high school movie trap of actors who have clearly been out of high school for over a decade playing students. They didn't want the audience to have to suspend their disbelief and take them out of the moment. The goal on *Superbad* was to avoid this entirely by casting actors who were under twenty years old.

The irony is that Hill could actually be seen playing a high school senior/college freshman that summer in *Accepted* opposite Justin Long and directed by Steve Pink. That role was Hill's most prominent to date, as *Knocked Up* hadn't come out yet. Hill plays a character named Sherman, who helps Long's character create a fake college on paper to convince his parents that he got accepted somewhere. Perhaps most memorably, he appears in a scene standing outside on campus in a giant hot dog costume as part of a pledge prank. As snickering college students walk by, Hill's character yells out,

"Ask me about my wiener!" It was abundantly clear that Hill was the breakout star of the film.

They hadn't really taken into consideration, however, the fact that Hill was presently in a movie playing a teenager. So with Hill out of the running, they continued to look for someone who seemed more age appropriate. But every time someone came in to read, the actor would lean too far into the sexual language and insert some explicit gestures. You have to walk a very thin tightrope with Seth, as venturing too far into the risqué territory takes away his likability and has him come off as pervy. The Seth character needed to have some manner of blissful ignorance to make clear that there was no malice behind even his harsher criticisms. Nobody they were seeing could pull that off.

As things intensified, Apatow was getting a little depressed on the set of *Knocked Up*, thinking, *The movie's greenlit. They will let us hire the wrong guy.* Everybody they were seeing in the auditions just felt like "the wrong guy." But the discussion kept coming back to Hill, who kept insisting that he could easily pull it off. There was something there that they just weren't seeing.[16]

With no good options coming their way, they decided to put Hill on tape to at least see what he could do with the role. Apatow went up to the actor on the set of *Knocked Up*—which was taping on the Sony lot despite being a Universal film—and instructed him to go into his trailer and shave really well so he could more easily pass as a teenager. Then, they'd all reconvene at Rogen's trailer so they could put Hill on tape.[17]

The close shave worked. Minus Hill's glasses, the character of Seth came to life right before the camera. Hill did the scene on the soccer field where Seth lays out his plan to buy alcohol for Jules's party that night. Throughout the course of his profanity-laced audition, you can almost feel the lightbulb going off from the other side of the camera. This was the moment when everyone realized just how much time they had been wasting when the answer was in front of them the entire time.

"She thought of me enough to decide that I was the guy that she was going to trust with the whole fun-ness of her entire party," Hill read in his audition, with Rogen reading the Evan part opposite him. "She wants me. She wants my fucking dick in her."[18]

So much of what transpired in that audition mirrors how it would go down in the actual film, from the dialogue to the mannerisms to even his inflections on certain lines. Hill also threw in some personal touches—with ad-libs such as "I might be allergic to pussy juice. I've never even tried it"—but it was clear as day by now. Like Cera, Hill was completely camera ready. Everyone immediately agreed. They'd found their guy.

The entire film rests on Seth's shoulders. He is the protagonist, but a risky one. In the wrong hands, such as those of all the previous auditioning actors, the dialogue can read as way too harsh and crude for a mainstream movie. After all, so much of Seth's dialogue for the majority of the first half of the film revolves around sexual fantasies. What they needed was an actor with enough vulnerability to offset that initial rough-around-the-edges vibe. They needed a performer with enough charisma to rise above the vulgarity.

There was an innocent quality to Hill, and he played to that strength. His Seth is clearly someone who has spent more time imagining what encounters with the opposite sex would be like than actually experiencing them for himself. His actions don't seem to be malicious. At one point in the script, he even admits that "I haven't been around that many drunk girls," further supporting the notion that this is all a fantasy he's built up in his head.

The filmmakers were so impressed with Hill's reading that Rogen dropped everything to take the tape up to Amy Pascal's office. Once he got up there, he played it for her, and her enthusiasm matched theirs. She told them to cast Jonah as Seth, and from there it was official.[19]

Because so much of the film hinges on Seth and Evan's relationship, it was imperative that the two actors playing the parts have natural chemistry. Luckily, that came pretty easily to Michael Cera and Jonah Hill. Prior to doing the film, they had actually met briefly at Henry Winkler's sixtieth birthday party as they were both mutual friends of Winkler's son, Max. They encountered each other again at a table read for another movie. Once Hill had the part in *Superbad*, he called Cera and left him a voicemail letting him know that they'd be working together.

After they found out they'd be working together, Apatow insisted that Hill needed to call Michael Cera and start spending every waking second with him until they shot the movie, to help build up their chemistry. They'd talk about the script, hang out at Canter's Deli, share their favorite movies, and play video games, among other similar things, to help break the ice. They also spent a lot of time rehearsing the film in Mottola's office, making sure their dynamic was as solid as possible before cameras ever started rolling. As a direct result, their chemistry emerged pretty early on.[20] "For us—for me—it was perfect casting," says Tolmach. "The chemistry between the two of them and the way that each of them embodied those different characters was so pitch-perfect."[21]

Even though both actors had completely different upbringings—with Hill being a California kid and Cera originally hailing from Canada—you immediately buy that these two have practically spent their entire lives together. The connection is just unexplainable—it's like magic. They each bring something different to the table in terms of their own comedic styles, but one never overpowers the other. Cera's hilariously understated performance pairs rather nicely with Hill's more animated character.

Hill and Cera were also careful from the beginning not to channel Rogen or Goldberg in the film. While the story is based on the writers' experiences—and the characters share their names—Seth and Evan are not intended to be a direct reflections of them. This allowed both actors the freedom to discover who these characters would be without feeling obligated to adhere to certain traits.

"It was more about seeming real instead of seeming like a bad impression of, seeming like just a person that actually exists," Cera said. "I don't think that was ever their intention was to have the characters sound like them or be like them."[22]

"Early on, we were hanging out at [Rogen's] house," Hill also said in an interview at the time of the film's release, "and we were playing video games, or something. And he goes, 'You're not going to do me, right?' I just told him, 'No.' That was the only time we ever discussed it. We are both unique in different ways. It was important to show that."[23]

As important as Seth and Evan obviously are to the plot, the role of Jules is undeniably just as crucial. Despite the fact that she only has roughly fifteen minutes of overall screen time, the whole movie hinges on her character. Or at least, it hinges on Seth's pursuit to get alcohol in order to hook up with her. Despite the hookup intentions, there's real sincerity behind Seth's desire. He's spent his entire adolescent life pining for her. Now this is his do-or-die moment, and it seems as if Jules is finally giving him the time of day. She is discussed and admired throughout the entire film, and that brings us as an audience closer to her character. There was a lot of pressure to get this casting right.

Certainly Jules is not your typical thankless, ditzy girlfriend part that conventional male screenwriters love to put into their films. She wasn't there to be scenery, nor was she a damsel in distress who was waiting around to find a young hero to buy her alcohol. Her character has a clear independent voice on the page. In a male-dominated movie, Jules needed to be someone who could hold her own among the boys. There had to be more to Jules's character than just existing as an object for Seth's affection. In her short time onscreen, she needed to be played by an actress who was so cool and down to earth that she could actually make that kind of impact.

If you were to look up the definition of a "down-to-earth actress" in the dictionary, you'd find Emma Stone's picture next to it. Originally hailing from Scottsdale, Arizona, Stone had her eyes set on an acting career ever since she was four years old. After performing in some local theater productions, she finally managed to convince her parents to let her move to Los Angeles to pursue an acting career. They arrived in 2004 when she was fifteen, and Stone hit the ground running on auditions.

She appeared in everything she could, from a reboot of *The Partridge Family* that wasn't picked up to an episode of Louis C.K.'s HBO sitcom, *Lucky Louie*. She had successfully gotten a role on a Fox series, *Drive*, that was canceled after seven episodes. None of these were the big break Stone had in mind. Determined as ever, she showed up to audition for *Superbad*.

Stone received a call from Allison Jones, who was a casting director she had auditioned for quite a few times with no success. Jones asked her to come in on a Saturday, telling her she thought she'd be great for the role of Jules in this new film. Stone went in and put herself on tape. She clearly made an impression, as they brought her in to take part in a table read, one that she would later recall neither Jonah nor Michael participating in.

Like everyone else who read the script, she immediately fell in love with it. Obviously, this is dangerous for any young actress—just because you've made it to a preliminary table reading doesn't mean the part is necessarily yours. This would also be her first film, so even though she kept reminding herself not to fall in love with the script in case she didn't the part, she couldn't help it. She got her hopes up and couldn't take her mind off it, even though she knew she may not get the role. For Greg Mottola, however, it was not even up for debate. Once he saw her on tape, he knew they had their female lead.

"I liked her from the first read," Mottola recalls. "I thought she's got this great voice. She's incredibly funny, she's really interesting, she's beautiful, but in an interesting way. I was shocked that she hadn't already been in a bunch of movies because she was so coy."[24]

Apatow adds about how Stone played the character in the audition, "I think we all thought she represented the kind of person who would appreciate Jonah. When you're young and in high school, you feel like nobody gets you. And then every once in a while there will be someone that was tuned into you in a way other people weren't. They have a similar sense of humor and they're smart and funny. She seemed to understand who the person is underneath the bravado."[25]

It wasn't necessarily a done deal, however, even with their stamp of approval. As Mottola recalls, the studio initially was looking for more of a traditional "teenage boy fantasy" type. The sort of peppy, busty blonde dream girl that would be the head of her sorority in college. That is a strong antithesis to the more chill aura that Stone gives off, and what the creative team was looking for with the character. Jules isn't written to just support the male characters. She's supposed to have depth and intellect that would make someone like Seth admire her all the more.[26]

Like Mottola, Apatow also pushed for Stone to get the part. In another case of being so certain of something that someone from the *Superbad* crew ran over to Pascal's office, Apatow did so with Emma Stone's tape. He put the tape in and told Pascal "She's it. She's gonna be a star."[27]

As for Tolmach and Pascal, they both remember being taken with her audition immediately. Tolmach watched her audition with his wife in the room, who—just as Apatow had—remarked, "Oh my God. That is a movie star. Hire that person." According to Mottola, there was one Sony executive who reportedly wasn't quite as sold as Tolmach and Pascal were, so the *Superbad* creatives told that executive to just have lunch with her and see for themselves. They did, and they immediately found her as charming as everyone knew they would.[28]

Still, before the part was hers, she would have to officially audition—yet again—with Jonah Hill this time. They went through the scene, and then when they were done, he started going off script and improvising. Stone—despite her nerves—took a deep breath and went along with it. That was how she sealed the deal. The part was hers, and she even managed to beat out some stiff competition for the role, including fellow future Oscar winner Jennifer Lawrence.

It isn't lost on Stone that her casting was because Allison Jones—for whom she had unsuccessfully auditioned multiple times previously—never forgot her. "I feel like it's a real testament to the power of casting directors and all of these auditions that you think are failed auditions and these parts you don't get. Sometimes someone remembers you, and asks you to come in for something and changes your whole life."[29]

Then you've got Evan's love interest, Becca. Martha MacIsaac was a Canadian actress living in Toronto when the call came in for her to audition for *Superbad*. She was in her early twenties and, like Cera, had been a child star. As a teenager, she starred in the CBC television series *Emily of New Moon*. The show lasted for four seasons, from 1998 until 2000. Following that, she did some more work in television and in films, mainly independent works, and all Canadian projects. She had never even done a comedy before.

The net for *Superbad* was cast pretty wide, even beyond the comedy world. The producers were essentially looking at anyone who could believably pass as a high school student. So MacIsaac put herself on tape for it while in Canada. Having done this for a wide variety of auditions, she didn't think much of it. She hadn't even read the script when she got the call a few weeks later to fly to LA to do a screen test.

When the script was given out at the audition, MacIsaac would later recall a lot of underage people there also reading for the roll. As a result, there was a large disclaimer on the script that said, "Make sure your child reads the whole script. If you're a parent, read the script. Your kid cannot just randomly audition for this." It was a smart tactic, as the last thing production would want is to find someone who is perfect for the role but wouldn't be able to do it because they feel that the script is too dirty. It's best that everyone knows what they're walking into.[30]

Her screen test in Los Angeles was opposite Michael Cera, which further drives Rogen's point home that Cera's full-time job back then was essentially to read with people for *Superbad*. Together, they read perhaps the most awkward scene you can imagine asking a young actress to read: the drunk scene with Cera in the bedroom where she attempts to sleep with him before throwing up all over the bed. This version somehow managed to be even filthier than the version that wound up in the film.

Filthy as the scene may be, it at least told every actress reading for the part what they were in for should they be cast. Naturally, MacIsaac nailed the screen test, and the part was hers. Once she finally got to read the full script, it certainly resonated with her. As someone who grew up in a small town, she definitely got the struggle of trying to procure alcohol from someone's parents and trying not to get caught.

When it came to the two main love interests, the only other concern was their hair color. Martha MacIsaac and Emma Stone were both brunettes at the time, though Stone is a natural blonde. When someone asked Apatow for his advice, he just said, "Well, maybe it could be red or something?"

"So we dyed her hair red, which I think she had never done before," says Apatow. "And since then, she has cursed me because now people love her with red hair and she's had to live with that for a lot of her adult life. It was a real tossed-off thought from someone who knows nothing about makeup and hair."[31]

There was one more love interest that they still needed to find. In the film, Nicola is Fogell's dream girl. Despite his awkward attempts to come on to her early in the film, he finally manages to dance with her at the party—after he gains confidence from being McLovin and has the wild night out with the cops, not to mention some good ol' liquid courage—before heading upstairs and briefly doing the deed.

Aviva Baumann was in her early twenties when she got the role of Nicola. She had worked on a few independent films prior to her *Superbad* audition, but this was also her first studio film. She initially came in to audition for other roles. However, they kept bringing her back in to read for Nicola instead.

As she recalls, "I think by the third time going in, I was like *The script is so good. They're trying to find a place for me. I'm going to give it all I got.* It was for Nicola and I read it the way they described it, they said she had on white pants and you could see the thong through her pants. I remember thinking to myself, *In my high school, that's when everyone was sagging their pants. You had your G-string showing above the pants.* So I just committed all the way."[32]

The final audition she did was for the dancing scene with Fogell at the party. On the way into the audition, she managed to get some attention from guys that she passed on the street, which she says helped boost her confidence. She leaned into that confidence and started dancing in the room, which everyone loved. The part was hers.

The next piece of the puzzle to figure out was the cops. Seth Rogen was technically the first person cast in the film, as once it became clear that Rogen had aged out of playing Seth, he became one of the two cops they had written, Officer Michaels. At a certain point, he was the only star they had attached to the film. Of course, this was before he actually broke out as a star, which didn't particularly help get the film sold.

"There were a few years where we were trying to sell the movie and I was just going to be the cop," Rogen later reflected. "And that was all we had, which made it even worse because we didn't even have a star. It was like we have a script and one of the guys playing like the fourth or fifth banana in the movie."[33]

When all of the pieces started coming together and it became clear that the film would get made, they had to find an Officer Slater. While trying to get *Superbad* made, Rogen took a small part in the film *You, Me, and Dupree*. There he met Bill Hader on the set and was immediately taken with him. They hit it off right away, and Rogen offered him the part—should they ever make it—of Officer Slater.

Apatow recalls, "Seth just came back and said to me 'I've found our new favorite person! It's this guy Bill Hader.' And that turned out to be true."[34]

By this point, Hader was still a rookie on *Saturday Night Live*, having just become a featured player in the fall of 2005. But he found himself quickly breaking out, thanks to his keen ear for doing impressions and dialects. Hader got the opportunity to show off his impressions on his first show, where he and Andy Samberg had an "impression-off" on Weekend Update. Hader did spot-on impressions of Peter Falk, James Mason, and Christopher Walken. Samberg, meanwhile, performed Jack Nicholson, Julia Roberts, and Christopher Walken where he made no attempt to change his voice whatsoever. But it was Hader's Vincent Price impression later that first season that quickly made him a fan favorite, once he started hosting Vincent Price holiday specials. That impression helped solidify what Hader could bring to the table, mixing a larger-than-life persona with solid comedic timing.

Over Christmas break in 2005, Hader met with Apatow for the first time. While Rogen had mentioned the film to Hader while on the *You, Me, and Dupree* set, they were still struggling to get it made. By the time Hader met with Apatow, not only was the film greenlit, but they knew he had to be their second cop. As Hader would recall, "Judd said 'So Seth and Evan said they met you and they enjoyed meeting you. They wrote this movie called *Superbad*, and there's a part for a cop that you're going to play.' I remember he didn't ask if I would play it. He said 'You're gonna play this.'"[35]

By this point, all of the principal parts had been cast. Well, almost all of them. There was still one role that would linger, serving as an uphill battle that would make every other casting dilemma look like a cakewalk in comparison. Fogell would prove to be the biggest challenge in casting that they would face on *Superbad*. Some would even end up calling this the most challenging casting process they'd ever endured over the course of their careers.

6

Who Is McLovin?

As hilariously written as the Seth and Evan characters are, it is clear as day that Fogell has the opportunity to easily steal every scene he's in—as long as the right actor is cast. And while finding someone to play Seth was a challenge, that search paled in comparison to the one they were about to embark on for Fogell.

Fogell—or McLovin—was not as easy to cast as you might imagine. True, the nerdy third banana had long been a staple of high school comedies. That sort of lovable loser became a much sought-after, predictable trope in Hollywood screenwriting. For decades, such secondary characters loomed large in film—such as Eugene in *Grease*—and TV—such as Screech Powers on *Saved By the Bell* and Steve Urkel in *Family Matters*. Even when they were given the opportunity to star in their own film—like in *Revenge of the Nerds*—the characters were still written in the same one-dimensional stereotypes with tape around their glasses. Aside from perhaps Anthony Michael Hall's character in *The Breakfast Club*—who lacked most of those cliché attributes—there hadn't really been much in terms of an evolution of "the nerd."

That's what makes a part like Fogell so enticing. It requires more than the simple caricature of having someone talk in a high-pitched, squeaky voice. Fogell isn't your standard nerd character with high-waisted pants and the highest IQ in the room. More often than not, you actually find yourself questioning Fogell's intellect. Even the Seth character wonders how Fogell got into Dartmouth. His decisions are seldom calculated and not especially well thought out, such as changing his name to "McLovin" on his fake ID. He's also the kind of guy who actually doesn't grasp how truly nerdy he is. As far as he's concerned, he's the hippest guy in the room—it's everybody else who's a nerd.

In the script, he is referred to as "one of those seniors who looks as if they're 13." Even though he's supposed to be the same age as Seth and Evan, they treat him more as an annoying little brother. As such, casting this unique type of character was something that no one involved with the production had any experience in. When you're dealing with something that nobody has any experience with, there's no frame of reference to point to. Essentially, you're just keeping your fingers crossed that the next person who walks into the room is going to be what you've been searching for.

"Nobody had any idea where [someone with Fogell's unique attributes] was going to come from," recalls Tolmach. "There were so many ideas. And it was such a specific thing for Seth and Evan. It was so loaded because these were real characters and real stories from their lives. [Fogell's] got an absurd level of confidence, of arrogance. That's the genius of it. He's the one character in the movie who never doubts himself. Everybody else is on some sort of journey of awkwardness and discovery. He is absolutely sure that he is the man and he is willing to dress like Aladdin."[1]

Trying to find the perfect Fogell sent the filmmakers to hell and back. Goldberg once referred to the casting process as "a *Twilight Zone* hole of madness." Rogen would later add, "We thought it was unactable. That's how hard it was. We started thinking, *We wrote a character that no one in the world can perform properly*, and we were literally just gonna change it. We were like, 'We have to completely rewrite it.'"[2]

The first step to getting to Fogell was bringing in every young actor in Hollywood to audition. One, Clark Duke, was a good friend of Cera's. While working on *Superbad*, Cera and Duke even created an internet show for the CBS website, titled *Clark and Michael*, in which they played fictionalized versions of themselves and featured many of their friends, including Hill. But Duke wasn't quite what they were looking for in regards to Fogell, though he'd later appear in the film during the scenes at Jules's party.

The more actors that came in, however, the more disillusioned the filmmakers got. There was nobody that seemed to match up with how Rogen and Goldberg envisioned the character. They had, so it seemed, painted themselves into a corner by making Fogell so niche. Now they had to find a way to get out of this corner, and fast. Time wasn't really on their side, and they had to adopt a new approach to casting the part.

One moment of realization came while shooting *Knocked Up*. During some downtime on the set, Apatow sat down with Rogen and Goldberg to watch a DVD of Fogell auditions. None particularly stood out. One of the kids auditioning was Dave Franco, the brother of *Freaks and Geeks* alumnus James Franco. As they were watching Dave's audition, Rogen immediately declared that he was far too good-looking for the part.

After watching a series of standard Hollywood types read for Fogell, Apatow finally turned to Rogen and Goldberg. "Look, you guys have to be hard, you have to be brutal with this," he told them. "You have to do open auditions in Vancouver and Chicago, see a thousand guys and look for the weird kid and see which one you can teach to act. They have to be the characters. We're not looking for the kids who can do Froot Loops commercials. This is not how we found Seth."[3]

Apatow had a point. Rogen was discovered for *Freaks and Geeks* in Vancouver, so he wasn't your typical Hollywood actor kid. What made him so intriguing was that he had a raw appearance and energy that was easily definable. He looked like the type of kid you'd actually know in high school, and he was cast because he was, by and large, the funniest person that came in. The same would have to be said about their future Fogell.

"In many, many cases, looks and humor don't go together," Allison Jones once said about her strategy as a casting director. "It's always a compromise if you go with the beauty queen and she's just not very funny. It hurts your project."[4]

So when you're not seeing any actors who are right for the part, the next logical step is to start looking at nonactors. For this, Jones widened the casting net. She started going around to local high schools and had them post ads that basically asked, "Are you interested in acting?" Email blasts were also sent out to the drama clubs at those schools. On top of that, Jones even embraced a new medium for finding kids that may not have been given much thought a few years earlier: the internet.

This unique approach included Jones creating a MySpace profile at the height of the social media platform's popularity. She then asked for high-school-aged kids to submit video auditions for the film. She received over four thousand responses from young hopefuls. While a rather foreign idea at the time, submitting audition videos online would soon become an integral part of the process, extending the field far beyond certain geographical limits. She was literally looking for anyone and everyone this time around.

Talk of the open casting calls made its way to one of the high school drama classes in the Los Angeles area. Someone in the class heard about an open audition for *Superbad*. He wound up telling his friend Christopher Mintz-Plasse about the open casting call the night before. Mintz-Plasse had barely acted in anything before, much less gone on an actual audition. He had done some acting in elementary and high school, essentially in short scenes. But he wasn't in the majority of his high school's plays. As Mintz-Plasse later put it, "My drama teacher never cast me in any. She didn't like me."[5]

The seventeen-year-old senior didn't even have a proper head-shot. In the days of the iPhone, it's a bit easier to fake that now—you've got access to a professional-looking headshot literally at your fingertips. But back in 2006, there were flip phones and not much else. That's exactly what Mintz-Plasse used to take his professional acting headshot. It couldn't be more bare-bones, but it worked. After seeing his amateur attempt at a headshot, Jones had a good feeling about him. According to Mintz-Plasse, she said, "Yup. You look good. Come on in."[6]

"I think I found McLovin; he's like Dill from *To Kill a Mocking-bird*," Jones, in an interview, later recounted telling director Greg Mottola. "You could tell he was a kid who probably had seen the inside of a locker."[7]

Mintz-Plasse managed to audition alongside his friends. Despite never having been on an audition before, he clearly had something of interest to Jones. He was the only one from his friend group who got a callback. For his second audition, he read with just Mottola. It went so well that they brought him back for a third reading with Hill and Cera. Also in the room that day was Mottola, Apatow, Rogen, Goldberg, Robertson, and Bill Hader.

It was that third callback with Hill and Cera that helped clinch the deal for Mintz-Plasse. The taped audition featured Mintz-Plasse going head-to-head with two working Hollywood actors who each had years of experience. One of these actors, Cera, had been going through the audition process for over ten years at this point, certainly making him the veteran in the room. Surprisingly, Mintz-Plasse effortlessly held his own, even under so much pressure.

The trio read the now-infamous fake ID scene, in which Fogell proudly shows off what he thinks is a "flawless" fake ID, which everyone else is quick to criticize. On the page, there's no better moment for the character of Fogell to shine than here. While much of the scene in the finished movie follows the script, Hill, at a certain point during the audition, started improvising. Impressively, Mintz-Plasse—who had an aura similar to Fogell's of someone without a care in the world—matched Hill's off-script banter.[8]

Mottola says that he "played it like he was clearly the coolest guy in the room and everyone else was a nerd and a loser. He was Dean Martin instead of Jerry Lewis." Others could immediately see that their long casting nightmare was likely over, as Mintz-Plasse was hitting every beat perfectly. At last, Rogen and Goldberg could start to see their creation coming to life before their eyes.[9]

Still, there was one person in the room who was advocating against Mintz-Plasse's casting, and that was Jonah Hill. From the jump, Hill took issue with Mintz-Plasse. One thing that made Mintz-Plasse stand out is that—as Fogell—it became clear that he wasn't going to take any crap from Seth or Evan. Everyone else that came in to audition had trouble holding his own against Hill, who makes no effort to hide his disdain for the character within the scene. As Seth would start dogging on them, the actors reading Fogell would sort of step back. Mintz-Plasse was the only one that wasn't intimidated by Hill. He was quick to dish it right back to him.

As Hill would hurl insults, Mintz-Plasse would throw them right back. At one point, Hill tells Mintz-Plasse during the audition, "I don't like you at all." Unafraid of Hill, Mintz-Plasse fires back, "That's all right. I don't like you." This was all much to the amusement of everyone else in the room. You can even hear Rogen's distinctive laugh roaring throughout the audition. It seemed like Hill was the only one who was less than impressed.[10]

As Apatow recalls, "Jonah said, 'I don't like that guy. I don't want him doing it.' And I said, 'That's exactly why we're hiring him. It couldn't be more perfect. The fact that it bothers you is exactly what we want.'"[11]

In recent years, Mintz-Plasse doesn't necessarily recall stepping over Hill's lines as Hill accused him of doing once the teenage actor left the room. To counter this, Apatow played the tape back and told Hill to find one instance of this happening. Hill could not. Mintz-Plasse certainly wasn't trying to step on anyone's lines, he was just trying to be himself. He was so excited to be there that he went around the room after the read and had everyone sign his script. He really didn't think he was going to get the part, so he was just trying to make the most of the experience.

It was that reading that sealed the deal, though. After months of painstaking auditions mixed with a fear that they'd never find anyone and would have to entirely rewrite the part, the search was over. Mottola called Mintz-Plasse to share the good news with him. When he got the call, Mintz-Plasse was at the gym working out. Mottola responded by saying, "You've got the part. Stop going to the gym." That was no problem for Mintz-Plasse, who hated going to the gym.[12]

As for the awkward energy between Hill and Mintz-Plasse, it wasn't immediately quashed once he got the part. The creatives behind the film didn't go out of their way to smooth things out, either. Instead, the two proceeded to butt heads, in a way that an older brother might with a somewhat annoying younger brother. This would not only help inform their characters but also allow both actors to deliver the best performance possible. You really find yourself buying into the fact that Seth doesn't like having Fogell around.

"Jonah, he didn't like my energy on set," Mintz-Plasse later said. "He definitely was a little on edge with me, which is totally fine because it works so well with the movie and also, who knows if I would have even gotten the part if he liked me or not. So, I'm kind of grateful he was annoyed with me."[13]

But Hill did come around to embrace Mintz-Plasse's presence in the film. As Apatow recalls, "Jonah very quickly fell in love with Chris. I just don't think he ever had that experience before where some kid who had never acted before just tried to tear him apart. He was just too perfect for it."[14]

It is also worth noting that Hill and Mintz-Plasse have since talked about the incident several times, and Hill later apologized. Mintz-Plasse never held any grudge and immediately quashed any beef that might have existed.

There was one other part, similar to Fogell, that Mottola recalls was really challenging to cast: Francis, the guy who hits Seth with his car and then takes Seth and Evan to an adult party. The character had to be played as off-putting and somewhat sleazy, but also pathetic and desperate. Each trait contradicts the other, which is what makes Francis work.

"We read a lot of really funny people for that" Mottola recalls. "That was a who's who of comedy folks. And no one could quite make it work. And we thought 'Well then I guess the scene doesn't work.' But then Joe Lo Truglio came in and he was so funny and so perfect, it was like 'Okay. We found our Francis.'"[15]

Lo Truglio had built up a solid reputation for himself with comedy fans. He was a founding member of the cult classic comedy troupe the State, and was featured in their self-titled short-lived MTV sketch series. His fellow alum from *The State* David Wain wound up casting Lo Truglio in *Wet Hot American Summer*, which has, alongside *The State*, also been dubbed a cult classic. Having Lo Truglio definitely earned *Superbad* some points with diehard comedy aficionados.

Finally, the filmmakers could breathe a sigh of relief. What initially seemed impossible was now a reality. They had their Fogell. After the decade-long struggle to get the film made and the just-as-stressful process of trying to cast it, all of the pieces were finally starting to fit. They had their green light, they had their cast, and now they could make *Superbad*.

7

Finding the Right Look

A key ingredient to any film's preproduction is determining the aesthetic that you're going for. From the overall vibe of the world you're creating to the music to the clothes the characters wear, there's a lot resting on making sure that these elements align. The title *Superbad* alone suggests a particular fondness for a certain era. Naturally, the James Brown song "Super Bad" from 1970 is the first thing that comes to mind. Despite the fact that the story is set in 2006—and not even the '90s, when Rogen and Goldberg were writing the film—there's a distinctive period that the film is trying to emulate.

Though Rogen and Goldberg were still in their early twenties when they were making *Superbad*, it's clear they have a lot of nostalgia for the comedies of the late '70s and early '80s. As film buffs from a young age, they had grown up watching a lot of those comedies. Apatow and Mottola were both a generation ahead of Rogen and Goldberg, so the fact that the film was a throwback definitely resonated with them as well.

"My upbringing in the '70s and '80s of more rebellious, off-color, *National Lampoon Animal House* teen comedies had gone away," Mottola recalls about watching studio comedies shift away from sheer raunchiness during the early '90s. "Largely because studios didn't want to put out R-rated movies for a young audience that may not be able to buy tickets and their parents may not take them. I thought, *That's a mistake. Because kids sneak into stuff, and nothing will stop them when they want a good laugh.*"[1]

While the main concern from the studios was the underage aspect, there is something to be said for returning to those raunch comedies of the '70s and '80s. After all, Apatow's recent run was proving that there was a hunger for more adult comedies, particularly among the younger generation, so it was clear that these films could be marketable in the modern age. Surely the success of those earlier Apatow films would help raise awareness. That's why they decided early on to go all in and lean into the '70s vibe. In the case of *Superbad*, you're pulled into that world before you even see a single frame of film. Underscored by the funky soundtrack, the filmmakers opted to utilize the 1970s Columbia Pictures logo instead of the modern-day equivalent. This tells you right away that you're in for a fun, nostalgic ride.

One way in which the filmmakers would be throwing things back was with the overall aesthetic. Once again turning to the *American Pie* films: they are brightly lit in a way that suggests *Well, it is a comedy, isn't it? It should be full of light and color.* On the flip side, *Freaks and Geeks*, which came out the same year as *American Pie*, couldn't look more different. Since the tone of *Freaks and Geeks* was admittedly quite a bit darker, the look of the show matched it. The show's creatives drew inspiration from their own upbringings rather than other high school shows. The halls of McKinley High School have a more vintage cinematic vibe than what you might find on a show like *90210*.

As a result, *Superbad* embraced earthy tones instead of vibrant colors or anything that would be conveyed as being too fun. There's a bit of sophistication in how the film is shot. Like the soundtrack, it feels like it's in stark contrast with just how dorky and out of touch these characters are.

Another defining factor in the film's look was bringing on Greg Mottola to direct. While Mottola did have experience directing comedies, his only theatrical film up to that point was an indie dramedy about a woman who travels to New York to confront her potentially philandering husband. The film won Mottola all sorts of praise in the independent world and was exactly why Rogen, Goldberg, and Apatow knew he'd be perfect. Much like hiring filmmaker David Gordon Green to direct *Pineapple Express*, the idea here was to hire a filmmaker who wasn't necessarily going to be looking for visual laughs. By having the film look more realistic only allows the organic jokes to land better. It feels like an actual film as opposed to your standard studio comedy. Just because the script is funny doesn't mean it has to look funny.

"We were just honored that he would do it," Rogen later said about getting Mottola to direct the film and bring his vision to it. "Any moment where you're thinking *This movie has a real quality*, that's because of him. Any shot that looks good, any music that goes along with anything, all Greg Mottola. We had none of that in our minds when we were writing it."[2]

One important asset of Apatow's productions was utilizing a lot of familiar faces not just on the screen but also behind the scenes. The producer always made it a point to surround himself with people he worked well with, pulling talent from the ever-growing roster he had built up over the course of his career. Apatow says of working with the same people, "It's hard to find people who are great at their jobs. So whenever you find someone who does fantastic work and is hopefully pleasant to deal with, you make a note and want to work with them again." Since *Superbad* would find the Apatow universe returning to high school for the first time since *Freaks and Geeks*, why not bring the man behind that camera on board for this newest venture?[3]

Russ T. Alsobrook got his start as a cinematographer on a variety of made-for-TV Disney movies, such as *The Shaggy Dog*, *The Computer Wore Tennis Shoes*, *Escape to Witch Mountain*, and *Freaky*

Friday. In 1992, Alsobrook first worked with Apatow when he was hired as the cinematographer on the short-lived—albeit beloved—*The Ben Stiller Show.* Later that decade, Alsobrook would shoot all episodes of both *Freaks and Geeks* and *Undeclared.* While working on the latter, he teamed up for the first time with Mottola. Naturally, when talk of *Superbad* came up, they called upon Alsobrook to shoot it.

"Greg and I had several meetings," says Alsobrook. "And one day we were talking about the look that would be appropriate. And he and I both agreed that we wanted it to be comedy noir. I've always thought that you develop the style to tell the particular story that you're shooting. And that's why I always thought of my style as being enhance naturalism, because I want it to look real. I want it to look like you're right there in the situation with the characters. And *Superbad* certainly has that feel to it."[4]

As Mottola had a strong connection to '70s and '80s comedies—which were anything but slick examples of filmmaking by today's standards—he was intent to make sure *Superbad* didn't look like the brightly lit modern teen comedies. He was conscious of adding some roughness and grit to the aesthetic, including utilizing handheld cameras. Coming from the world of independent films, with lower budgets, he was pretty familiar with such methods. Like *Freaks and Geeks*, *Superbad* was going to have a more natural feel, sort of like something you might see from Hal Ashby or John Cassavetes.

Much of the plot of *Superbad* takes place at night, which is also going to influence the overall vibe. As Alsobrook puts it, the film is kind of a "dark voyage." So they opted for a raw, indie feel, despite being done on a film studio's dime. This was something everyone involved immediately agreed on, ensuring that *Superbad* would have a more serious look.

Night shoots are challenging—after a certain point, you're acting on pure adrenaline. There's an added layer of giddiness, but also camaraderie with your fellow cast and crew members. While the rest of the world is asleep, you're bonding over creating something you truly believe in. To be fair, shooting so late is much easier when you've got a younger cast. In the case of *Superbad*, none of the actors were older than thirty. In fact, Bill Hader was technically the elder statesman as far as performers went, having just turned twenty-eight a few months prior. Unlike most night shoots, Mottola doesn't really remember racing against the sunrise in order to get everything he needed.

For as much as the film embraced nostalgia, there was one technique they employed that wasn't just modern but rather cutting edge at the time: shooting digitally. Not only was this a first for an Apatow production, but the technology was also still in its infancy as far as the industry was concerned. While the idea of shooting on digital may be commonplace now, in 2006 film stock was still king. Of course, the pendulum would eventually swing completely in the other direction, but the number of films shot on digital was relatively low back then.

"Essentially we were guinea pigs for Judd," Mottola says. "He was trying to decide if he should switch to digital, because you can shoot such long takes. And he loves to keep the camera rolling and talk the actors through things and improvs and never call cut, which is harder to do on film. Interestingly, Judd has continued to shoot on film. The rest of us have moved on to digital."[5]

Dating as far back as the mid-'90s, digital films were reserved for very low-budget fare. And even when things were shot on digital, it essentially yielded the same result as gathering a bunch of talented actors around and shooting a movie on your camcorder. New Line Cinema was the first major film studio in 2000 to release a movie shot entirely on digital. That movie was Spike Lee's *Bamboozled*, which he shot that way to keep the budget low.

By 2002, however, George Lucas utilized digital to shoot *Star Wars: Attack of the Clones*, which is generally accepted by many as the first blockbuster to adopt the new medium. Not far behind him was Robert Rodriguez, who used digital to shoot all of his movies starting with *Spy Kids 2*. Still, prior to 2006, the format was used sparingly, and only to achieve a specific look that the filmmaker felt couldn't be done on film stock. So shooting *Superbad* this way still felt a bit like walking into the unknown, even though it had been done before by multiple productions.

It just so happened that Alsobrook had experience shooting on digital. The film he did right before *Superbad* was *Reign Over Me*, which was directed by Mike Binder and starred Adam Sandler and Don Cheadle. For that film, he utilized the Panavision Genesis camera, which has a 35-millimeter chip so it can retain the same feel and aspect ratio that you'd get with film. Due to how *Reign Over Me* turned out—as well as Alsobrook's familiarity with the camera—*Superbad* was also shot on the Panavision Genesis. This helped achieve the unique aesthetic they were going for, and the Genesis allowed for a subtle blend of the modern and the vintage. The fact that the Genesis didn't have the crispy, digital look like many of those early adapters did was something else that drew Alsobrook to using it.

Just as crucial to finding the person to capture the look was finding the person who could help create the physical world. Just like Mottola, Alsobrook, and so many others who were working on the film, the production designer, Chris Spellman, also had ties with the Apatow world. Spellman first crossed paths with Apatow when he was a set decorator on *Heavyweights*. Like Alsobrook, he also worked on *Freaks and Greeks*. This meant that Spellman had already proven that he had experience creating a realistic universe for the characters to exist within, much as he had done with the Weir home on *Freaks and Geeks*.

A few years after *Freaks and Geeks*, Apatow approached Spellman about being a set decorator again on *Knocked Up*. He had served as a set decorator on a variety of projects over the years, including *The*

Big Lebowski, Grosse Pointe Blank, Magnolia, Orange County, Daddy Day Care, and *Anger Management.* But by 2006 he was looking to get away from set decorating and focus on production design instead. So Apatow came up with a creative alternative offer.

Spellman recalls, "He said, 'Look, I have this other project that I'm going to produce right after that, and you'll be the designer on it.' I felt like it was the dangling carrot. I talked to him and I said 'It doesn't quite work like that. What if the director doesn't want to hire me?' And his plan was he was going to treat it like one of his television shows. He was going to hire all of the department heads."[6]

This type of promise is made all the time in show business. That doesn't mean it will inevitably happen. However, Apatow was true to his word. While working on *Knocked Up,* Spellman received the script for *Superbad.* As he read through it, the first thing he wondered was *How do we make this experience for every high school kid?* Spellman had gone to high school in the '70s, so he was able to effectively bring that authentic vibe the film was going for to the table. This meant utilizing a lot of those same earthy tones Alsobrook was after to help ground things. Big flashy colors weren't going to work for this project, so they went above and beyond to avoid those.

Another hurdle the filmmakers had to deal with involved the alcohol. A film like *Superbad* obviously would necessitate a lot of alcohol use on screen. The vast majority of the alcohol would be handled—and consumed—by underage characters. Due to the legal complications, no alcohol company was champing at the bit to have their brand featured in the film. So the filmmakers had to find a way around it.

The solution was to bring in a graphic artist named Ted Haigh to create all of the fake alcohol labels that you see in the film. In addition to being a graphic designer, Haigh is also an expert when it comes to mixology, so much so that his nickname is Dr. Cocktail. He even wrote a book on the history of the cocktail, *Vintage Spirits and Forgotten Cocktails: From the Alamagoozlum to the Zombie and Beyond; 100 Rediscovered Recipes and the Stories behind Them.* Haigh had to get creative in balancing novelty with recognizability. For instance, instead of Mike's Hard Lemonade, you've got Kyle's Killer Lemonade. Close enough that you know what it's supposed to be, but different enough that the filmmakers won't get sued.

Naturally, using all of your own liquor bottles slows things down when you're filming on location. The film crew had to go in and remove all of the preexisting bottles in the convenience store, the liquor store, and the supermarket so they wouldn't appear on camera. Then they'd replace them with their own bottles for the shoot before swapping everything back out again when filming wrapped. Sadly, Kyle's Killer Lemonade or Gold Slick Vodka were never actually on the shelves during normal business hours.

The filmmakers weren't just limited by their alcohol brands, either. Pepsi demanded a major stipulation in order to have their products displayed in the film: any character in the film was allowed to interact with and drink their products, except for Seth. For instance, in the lunchroom scene, you'll see Evan with a Sierra Mist. In the background, you can spot an Aquafina bottle, another Pepsi product. Seth, however, is drinking from a milk carton, a choice that also helps paint the character as sort of an outsider. Sony requested similar stipulations, and thus Seth was barred from playing any Sony video games onscreen—which is odd, considering it's a Sony film. The laundry detergent bottle that Seth uses to carry alcohol out of the adult party looks like a Tide bottle, but it isn't. Tide wasn't in a hurry to have an underage character smuggle alcohol in one of its containers. Filmmakers have to make these kinds of concessions that the general audience typically won't pay attention to.[7]

And how were the characters even going to get the alcohol? Fogell's fake ID has gone on to become an iconic fixture in pop culture, but at the time, it was just a hilarious way to move the plot along. Spellman was tasked with fleshing out some of the more memorable details that were on his ID. "In the first script," Spellman says, "it just said McLovin had a fake driver's license. But it's my job to say *Okay, where is this license from? What street does he live on?* I pitched in one of the meetings 'What if we made him from someplace like Hawaii or Alaska?' And they started cracking up laughing."[8]

Mottola, however, recalls that Hawaii was his idea. When he went online to look up a variety of fake IDs to figure out where the fictional McLovin would hail from, he realized that the Hawaii ID had a rainbow in the background. This made him laugh, so it went into the script. As for the joke that McLovin was an organ donor, Mottola recalls it coming up during preproduction.

So much of how the characters dress is based on their individual personalities. When you've got a film that mostly takes place in the span of one incredibly long day, extra special attention has to be paid to the wardrobe, as the actors will all be wearing the same thing for practically the entire film. The clothes also have to match the world being created, which in this case was essentially a throwback without being a period piece. This meant that the costumes had to be specifically reminiscent of the '70s while not looking dated (save for Fogell's vest, which purposely clashes with the aesthetic).

"I'm not really motivated by fashion," said the film's costume designer, Debra McGuire. "I'm much more interested in [film], even though I'd been a fashion designer before I started with costume design. It's a very different world. So, we're dealing with characters. The most important thing is to be able to convey a story that's intended by both the writer and director."[9]

McGuire has been a highly sought after costume designer dating back to the early '90s. She is perhaps best known for her work on *Friends*. Like practically everyone else working on *Superbad*, she first came into the Apatow world on *Freaks and Geeks* before collaborating with him again on *Undeclared, Anchorman, The 40 Year-Old Virgin*, and *Knocked Up*.

"The big thing we thought about was, we had the image on the T-shirt that I wear in the school," said Hill. "We all thought that should be an iconic image. Whatever it was. There were a lot of different things. The Richard Pryor one, I couldn't have been happier with that. That shirt had to kind of describe who this guy is. He's kind of funny, he likes cool things. He is interested in old-school stuff. We had a lot of different versions of that shirt, and that is the one we landed on. There were a lot of discussions about it. It was really important to make that outfit kind of cool seeming. It looks ridiculous, but in a way it ends up being kind of cool by the end of the movie."[10]

There's also the backstory to Seth's main outfit he wears throughout the majority of the film. Because his car is towed and he can't go home, he has to borrow clothes from Evan's dad. That explains the really funky-looking shirt-and-pants combo, which is obviously not something your average high schooler in 2006 would've generally worn.

All the way up until production, the script was still getting tweaked in order to find the right tone. This happens to every movie script: changes happen all the way up until the cameras start rolling, even after that. For instance, there is a version of the *Superbad* script dated July 20, 2006, just two months before production started in September. In this version, a significant number of changes have yet to be made. For instance, Becca is still named Helen. It's also missing the filthy home economics gestures, as well as large chunks of iconic dialogue. Some of these things didn't get adjusted until the zero hour.

And this doesn't even account for the ad-libbing. Apatow, as usual, left the door open for improvisation. Never shy about giving their actors the freedom to add things, the filmmakers even sought information for the film's dialogue. Rogen would ask people

"What's a story from when you were in high school?" If not the stories themselves, then at least the motivation behind them would inform the overall script. A line of communication existed between the writers and actors that is rare within most productions. A lot of times, writers aren't overly involved by the time a project is cast, and if they are, a lot of times it's behind the scenes. But the presence of Rogen and Goldberg was felt every step of the way. They wanted to make the film as good as possible, and if feedback from their cast could inspire the script and help make it that much better, then they were totally open to it.[11]

Despite the open communication and the encouragement to ad-lib, things were pretty close to what you see in the finished film by the time they got to the final table read stage. As Apatow recalls, "We did a table read of it a couple of weeks before we started shooting, and it was the most riotous table read we've ever done. It was all there. And we all laugh about the fact that people think a lot of it is improvised. But when you watch the film and read along with the final draft of the script, the vast majority of it was in the script. It was one of those situations where not being able to get it made [for a long time] led to a very strong and thought-through draft."[12]

As always, though, there was room for improvisation. It wasn't just limited to on set, either. The rehearsal process had a certain looseness to it that allowed for actors to strike gold in their banter that wound up in the script. It's not unlike what Apatow had Rogen and Jessica Campbell do for *Freaks and Geeks*. The method had worked for them so many times before—why mess with the winning recipe now?

Hill said, "The thing about Judd [Apatow]'s process, also with *Knocked Up*, was rehearsing and recording the rehearsal. So, essentially allowing the actor to write what would be most natural and true to them. You know what I'm saying? So, hopefully our things don't sound like it's acting or sound like it's being read off a script as opposed to sounding like it actually happened or that you were talking about something that was actually going on in your life."[13]

Having a film that allows for so much improvisation really gives the actors the added freedom to find the characters themselves. While they are always going to be truthful to what's on the page, when you've got characters that you have to share such a deep connection with in order to make it believable, there has to be room to play.

This was the moment that Rogen and Goldberg had waited over a decade to get to. The impossible was finally happening. On September 18, 2006, cameras would start rolling on their high school epic. It just goes to show that no matter how many times people tell you something is never going to happen, you've got to trust your instincts. For Rogen and Goldberg, there would never have been a *Superbad* if they hadn't trusted theirs.

8

A Once-in-a-Lifetime Experience

Scheduling is key when it comes to a film shoot. Everybody involved in a production has the same goal: "Make it as easy as possible on yourself and try not to go over budget." Typically, you'll want to leave some of the more challenging sequences for later in the shoot. This allows everyone on the crew time to find their rhythm and see how they gel. Even though a majority of the cast and crew were already pretty used to one another by the time they made *Superbad*, of course.

That didn't happen here. Instead, they opted to kick things off—literally—with the soccer field sequence, which is the foundation that the film is essentially built upon. This is perhaps the most dialogue-heavy scene in the entire film and is an exhausting tour de force for Hill. Seth has to lay the groundwork for the plot in an expletive-heavy rant about why this is the night that he and Evan will finally get to sleep with their dream girls. It's eight pages of dialogue, all of it is exposition, and it's most definitely going to appear front and center in the trailer.

There was so much they had to cover (in addition to having to work out the first-day-of-shooting kinks) that they inevitably wouldn't get to everything. As Mottola recalls, "There was that sense of 'We're already behind and it's the first day.' I said to Judd 'I want to try to find a way to come back and do more of this if we can squeeze it in another day.'" On the first day of his first studio movie, Mottola was already asking for more time. Luckily, Apatow understood his reasoning and fully supported it. Mottola knew that it could be better, and they managed to carve out some time in the schedule to make it happen. A lot of the close-ups that you see in the film are from later reshoots because Jonah was able to get a better grasp on the Seth character and how to play him.

One idea that was floated about in order for the film to be shown on TV and on airplanes was to have the cast do censored takes after the dirtier scripted ones to create a clean version of the film. This is supposed to help the film translate to audiences that aren't going to see it in theaters or run out to rent it. Of course, this didn't make anybody's life any easier—when you've got a movie like *Superbad*, there's a *lot* of censoring that has to be done. Expecting the actors to redo the same scene and deliver the same performance but without the curses was a tall order.

In the theatrical version, one of Seth's more descriptive lines is "She's got an older brother. And she could've asked him, but she asked me. She looked me in the eyes and said 'Seth, Mom is making a pube salad, and I need some of Seth's own dressing.' She's DTF. She's down to fuck, man. P in vagi. She wants to *fuck*, man. And tonight is the night that fucking is an actual possibility."[1]

Some movies may have just tried to dub over the more questionable lines for TV. But when you've got a monologue that gets as explicit as Seth's does, it would be nearly impossible to redub anything and have it match up with Hill's mouth. It would be enough to make any censor's head spin. So as far as Apatow was concerned, this was a good way to get ahead of any post-production headaches while they were making the film.

"We realized early in making these types of films that they always wind up on ABC or basic cable and then you wind up in an ADR session replacing every curse with something that is airable," says Apatow. "I would always try to get the director to force everyone to do one take where all the curses were replaced that we could tolerate if it was on ABC or basic cable. And on *Superbad*, everyone revolted against me. They didn't really want to do that."[2]

The mood on set wasn't exactly cheerful when it came to the TV-safe lines. Still, they gave it their best shot. In between takes, there were lots of debates about just what could be changed to make the exchange "TV friendly." "She wants me. She wants to get with me," is one possibility that was thrown out. Another possible alteration was "She wants to party with me inside her." Instead, they settled on "She's got an older brother, okay? She could've asked him, but she asked me. She looked me in the eyes and she said, 'Please do this for me.' She wants to hook up. She wants to hook up, and tonight is the first night that hooking up is finally like an actual possibility."[3]

Hill recounted after shooting the scene, "They go 'Do a clean take,' and it was one of the most difficult things I've ever done, because almost every other word I had to change . . . I guess from 'pussy' to 'vagina' was one that worked maybe. 'Fuck' to 'shoot.'"[4]

"Our schedule could not absorb shooting two completely different movies at the same time," says Mottola. "It'd be like them shooting the Spanish-language *Dracula* at the same time that they're shooting the original *Dracula*. You need a second crew and another director." Given the film's $20 million budget, this was obviously cost prohibitive. It was one crew shooting what would turn out to be two separate movies.[5]

They tried again to create TV-safe lines for a different scene. As Seth and Evan are leaving the convenience store before school, Seth says "You're misunderstanding me, okay? I'm not trying to insult her. I'm just saying that she looks like a good fucker, okay? She looks like she could take a dick. Some women pride themselves on their dick-taking abilities." Evan asks, "Dick-taking abilities? Do you think that's a good thing to say about someone?" Seth fires back, "The fucked up thing is, I actually do, okay? If some woman tried to compliment me on my dick-giving abilities, I'd be psyched."[6]

For the TV-safe line, they opted for "You're misunderstanding me, okay? I'm not trying to insult her. I'm just saying it looks like she gets filthy, okay?" Evan says "Gets filthy? You think that's like a nice thing to say about someone?" "The crazy part is, I actually do. If some woman tried to tell me 'Hey, I bet you get filthy, sir,' I'd be like 'Awesome.'" While both variations have the same premise, the clean version just doesn't pack the same punch. The point of the scene is Evan calling Seth out for saying something so horribly profane and offensive about his love interest. Saying that she seems like she likes to "get filthy" wouldn't necessarily cause a teenage boy to get angry at his best friend. It's just not as graphic.[7]

As time went on, it became more and more challenging to try and remove the swear words. It also took attention away from making the best theatrical version of the film possible. Not only that, but with clean takes the film was drifting in the opposite direction of what Seth and Evan set out to do with *Superbad*, which was to represent how teenagers actually talked. It would mean that there would be a PG-13 version of the film out there, similar to what DreamWorks tried to get them to make years earlier. At a certain point, the filmmakers realized that the idea of doing TV-safe lines was just too difficult and expensive a task for this film, particularly with a shooting schedule that was barely over forty days. So they eventually shifted their focus away from the idea, and that was that.

That Apatow was able to begin shooting a simultaneous censored version of *Superbad* illustrates how much sway he had with the studios: they more or less trusted what he was doing and kind of left him alone to do his own thing. It's only this kind of creative freedom that can truly allow a unique project like *Superbad* to thrive. There wasn't a sense that the studio was breathing down Apatow's neck during production or trying to micromanage things. The last thing you want is too many cooks in the kitchen.

"Judd is very good at making studios feel like the best result that they can get is if they don't really ask a lot of questions or get in the way," says Robertson. "That we're going to do our best work uninterrupted. By that point, we had proved that we could do that. And we were working at a budget level that was low enough that I think people kind of stayed out of our way. Sony was very supportive. They got the joke. We felt pretty safe making the movie we wanted to make."[8]

"It was the beginning of an incredible run for us," Tolmach recalls about the relationship the studio fostered with Apatow, as well as Rogen and Goldberg, during this period. "There was just a lot of business that came out of this relationship. It's something that's very meaningful to the studio."[9]

It also didn't hurt that the rest of the film crew, not just Apatow, also had a proven track record you could point to. While *Knocked Up* hadn't come out yet, things seemed to be on a roll with *Anchorman*, *The 40 Year-Old Virgin*, and *Talladega Nights*. With Apatow, Robertson, Rogen, Goldberg, and Mottola, everyone seemed to be doing great work and making the studio boatloads of money in the process. When you've got commercial success on your side, the studio tends to be a little more at ease with the creators.

Within the first few days of filming, Michael Cera came down with food poisoning. Cera has described this as the sickest he's ever been in his life. As Evan is present in the vast majority of the film, practically nothing could be shot without him, save for scenes with Fogell and the officers. However, *Saturday Night Live* had just kicked off its latest season, leaving Hader unavailable until a few weeks into the shoot.

So they did the only thing they could do: they took an insurance day. Every film production has a certain number of days set aside for extenuating circumstances. You still want to do everything in your power to avoid them, as they are going to cost the production money and you'll have one less day of safety net. But if you need to utilize them, they're available. As Rogen later said, "They don't like giving you insurance days. And I remember Evan had to drive to Michael Cera's house and confirm that he was in dire enough condition."[10]

That wasn't the only time Cera would wind up with an illness or injury on the set of the film, either. On a lunch break during the filming of the convenience store scene, Cera, Hill, and MacIsaac went to a local park and started climbing a tree. As Cera went to sit on a branch, it came up and cut his lip open. Thankfully, the injury was minor and didn't set production back at all.

Rogen missed the first week of filming with a case of shingles. Because Mintz-Plasse had never had chicken pox before, Rogen was deemed highly contagious and had to stay away from set. Luckily, since all of his scenes were with Bill Hader, his absence didn't affect the schedule, although it probably drove him crazy that he couldn't be there to watch his passion project finally come to life.

Superbad was filmed all throughout Southern California. The high school scenes were shot in September at El Segundo High School, which was an actual functioning high school in session: the crew had to halt production every time they'd hear the bell ring. It would have been next to impossible to find an operating high school that could accommodate production and close down for filming. The cost for building new sets for what would be just a few minutes of screen time also wasn't in the budget. So they had to make do with what resources they had.

Both the filmmakers and the students served as distractions for one another. Many of the students recognized Hill from *Accepted*, which had just opened a few months earlier. Because of his hot dog scene in that film, he endured countless "Ask me about my wiener!" shouts from the high schoolers who saw him. It got old pretty fast.[11]

The various liquor stores and supermarkets that they shot in definitely serve as some of the film's most iconic locations. One of the liquor stores is literally down the street from Jonah Hill's parents' house, where he grew up. Hill was basically reenacting the struggle of trying to get alcohol in essentially the same neighborhood where he would've been trying to get alcohol in high school.

"We would just drive far out and look for the seediest-looking liquor store," Hill once said of his quest to find alcohol as a teenager. "I looked like I was fourteen when I was sixteen, and I would obviously not be twenty-one, and they would sell me alcohol."[12]

As for how he approached the character of Seth, Hill tried to find a way to incorporate the authentic emotions or feelings that he remembered from that age (although he has noted that Seth is angrier than he was in high school). But at the heart of Seth, Hill definitely went all in on trying to invoke that high school spirit. Being so close to his parents' house actually came in handy for Hill, as he utilized the proximity to tap into the feeling of being in high school again. It helped him form a deeper connection with the character. Despite only being four years removed from graduating when they made *Superbad*, Hill took a method approach to bring him back to that place.[13]

"I had a lot of conversations with Greg and Judd about not being who I am now, to not have any traces of myself now," Hill said at the time of the film's release. "So I moved back in with my parents. I stayed in the same bedroom where I lived in high school, which was torturous, as you can imagine. I would go through my old yearbooks and look through my stuff and try and get back to a place where [I was]—and it did, I started feeling the same lack of privacy."[14]

Hill going so far out of his way to get into the proper headspace makes sense. This was an opportunity that every actor dreams of, to be the lead in a movie. So much of the film rests on his shoulders, as he has to deliver monologue after filthy monologue in several scenes. The fact that it was happening to him at such a young age just made those stakes even higher. It helped that he could turn to Rogen for advice, who had gone through a similar experience a month prior to

Superbad's production with *Knocked Up*. Rogen advised Hill to "just pretend like you're not the lead in the movie. Just play it like you would play your other roles."[15]

On a lot of film sets, the director will hang out by what is called video village to watch what the camera is picking up in real time. Mottola liked to get away from video village when he could, so he had the crew set up a monitor for him right next to the camera. Mottola began to notice that Hill would occasionally look over to him mid-take, as if thinking *What did Greg think of that?* Mottola made sure to get out of his line of sight from that point forward to alleviate some of the pressure Hill was feeling.

Hill wasn't the only person who went out of his way to get into character prior to production: Rogen and Hader ended up going on a police ride-along in South Los Angeles. When you see their police officers on screen, you may find yourself thinking, *Well this is funny, but there's no way that these characters could actually exist in the real world.* But what Rogen and Hader discovered is that they actually do exist.

Rogen declares that the cop they were paired with was "the worst cop on Earth. Or maybe an incredibly average cop." He continues, "A lot of the attitude honestly that we had in the movie was based off of this guy. He didn't seem to give a fuck about anything. He didn't care. He was antagonizing people, bothering people. He saw it as funny. Everything we do in the movie was within the capabilities of how this guy we went on a ride-along with would potentially act. We were like 'Why'd you become a cop?' and he was like, 'Ya know. You just run around and tackle motherfuckers. It's fun!'"[16]

They were supposed to shadow the cop all night as he was on the job, going from 10 p.m. until 4 a.m. But after forty-five minutes, they decided they'd had enough. Rogen eventually concludes, "As dumb and as irresponsible as we maybe were thinking of playing them, we could have them be one hundred times dumber and more

Figure 1 Evan (Michael Cera), Fogell (Christopher Mintz-Plasse), and Seth (Jonah Hill) watching pornography in Evan's basement during their "incredible, unbelievable" Saturday night. COLUMBIA PICTURES / PHOTOFEST © COLUMBIA PICTURES, PHOTOGRAPHER: MELISSA MOSELEY

Figure 2 Director Greg Mottola behind the scenes of *Superbad*. COLUMBIA PICTURES / PHOTOFEST © COLUMBIA PICTURES, PHOTOGRAPHER: MELISSA MOSELEY

Figure 3   Producer Shauna Robertson, cowriter Evan Goldberg, and actor Jonah Hill in between takes on the set of *Superbad*. COLUMBIA PICTURES / PHOTOFEST © COLUMBIA PICTURES, PHOTOGRAPHER: MELISSA MOSELEY

Figure 4   Seth (Jonah Hill) and Evan (Michael Cera) wait for Fogell outside the liquor store while he illegally buys alcohol for Jules's party. COLUMBIA PICTURES / PHOTOFEST © COLUMBIA PICTURES, PHOTOGRAPHER: MELISSA MOSELEY

Figure 5   Officer Slater (Bill Hader) and Officer Michaels (Seth Rogen) respond to the "McLovin" on Fogell's ID after the liquor store robbery. COLUMBIA PICTURES / PHOTOFEST © COLUMBIA PICTURES, PHOTOGRAPHER: MELISSA MOSELEY

Figure 6   Becca (Martha MacIsaac) encourages Evan (Michael Cera) to drink more at Jules's party before they go upstairs. COLUMBIA PICTURES / PHOTOFEST © COLUMBIA PICTURES, PHOTOGRAPHER: MELISSA MOSELEY

Figure 7   Seth (Jonah Hill) and Jules (Emma Stone) are partnered up to make tiramisu in home economics class after Seth complains about having to do double the work on his own. COLUMBIA PICTURES / PHOTOFEST © COLUMBIA PICTURES, PHOTOGRAPHER: MELISSA MOSELEY

Figure 8   Fogell (Christopher Mintz-Plasse) and Nicola (Aviva Baumann) dance together at Jules's party before their hookup. ENTERTAINMENT Pictures / Alamy Stock Photo

Figure 9   Officer Michaels (Seth Rogen) raises his hands in surrender when Officer Slater tells him not to shoot a perp. "Stop him, McLovin!" COLUMBIA PICTURES / PHOTOFEST © COLUMBIA PICTURES, PHOTOGRAPHER: MELISSA MOSELEY

Figure 10   Producer Judd Apatow watching a take on the set of *Superbad.* COLUMBIA PICTURES / PHOTOFEST © COLUMBIA PICTURES, PHOTOGRAPHER: DARREN MICHAELS

Figure 11   Writers Seth Rogen and Evan Goldberg pose with their cinematic counterparts Jonah Hill and Michael Cera on the set of *Superbad.* COLUMBIA PICTURES / PHOTOFEST © COLUMBIA PICTURES, PHOTOGRAPHER: MELISSA MOSELEY

Figure 12   Fogell (Christopher Mintz-Plasse) in his suede vest, ready to use his fake ID. It's futile, and Seth tries (and fails) to steal the booze instead. COLUMBIA PICTURES / PHOTOFEST © COLUMBIA PICTURES, PHOTOGRAPHER: MELISSA MOSELEY

Figure 13   Shirley (Laura Seay) and Jules (Emma Stone) ask Seth to get them alcohol for their upcoming party. ENTERTAINMENT PICTURES / ALAMY STOCK PHOTO

Figure 14   Officer Slater (Bill Hader) and Officer Michaels (Seth Rogen) are shocked at McLovin's ability to take down a perp. RGR COLLECTION / ALAMY STOCK PHOTO

Figure 15 Seth (Jonah Hill) reveals that he used to have a crippling addiction to drawing dicks. AJ Pics / Alamy Stock Photo

Figure 16 Evan (Michael Cera) finds out that Becca exposed Seth's dick-drawing addiction. His childhood was ruined as a result. Entertainment Pictures / Alamy Stock Photo

Figure 17 Fogell (Christopher Mintz-Plasse) gets IDed after the assault in the liquor store. Columbia Pictures / Photofest © Columbia Pictures, Photographer: Melissa Moseley

Figure 18 Fogell (Christopher Mintz-Plasse) reveals his "McLovin" pseudonym to Seth (Jonah Hill) and Evan (Michael Cera). It was between that and Muhammad. COLUMBIA PICTURES / PHOTOFEST © COLUMBIA PICTURES, PHOTOGRAPHER: MELISSA MOSELEY

Figure 19 Michael Cera, Jonah Hill, and Christopher Mintz-Plasse promoting the film at Dave & Busters. SCOTT WEINER / MEDIAPUNCH / ALAM STOCK PHOTO

Figure 20 Evan (Michael Cera) and Seth (Jonah Hill) on the ground after Officer Slater (Bill Hader) and Officer Michaels (Seth Rogen) hit Seth with their cop car. COLUMBIA PICTURES / PHOTOFEST © COLUMBIA PICTURES, PHOTOGRAPHER: MELISSA MOSELEY

irresponsible, and it would be firmly within the reality of what a cop is it seems."[17]

Like how Rogen drew upon his own experience with cops growing up—and imagining them drinking all their alcohol after confiscating it—Hader also brought some experience into the mix. When Hader was growing up in Tulsa, Oklahoma, there was a cop who would always bust kids for underage drinking and would make them pick up beer cans in the park as punishment. This particular cop had kind of an obnoxious attitude and wore glasses, both of which Hader brought to his portrayal of his character.[18]

Early on during production, the filmmakers also brought in a police consultant to be present for the cop scenes. The consultant, however, kept telling Rogen and Hader that what they were doing was wrong and not at all accurate. He wound up being let go that first day. "We don't care if it's accurate," Rogen told the consultant at the time. "As soon as reality infringes on what we think is funny, that's when we stop caring." Plus, Rogen and Hader already had a strong sense of how to play the characters after just that short ride-along. They knew that—accurate or not—the depiction at least aligned with what they had personally witnessed.[19]

The film had a packed forty-day production schedule, which for most studio films—particularly one that had as much going on as *Superbad* did—would be considered tight. Fortunately, Mottola came from the indie film world and was prepared for anything, even though nothing went terribly wrong on set. With the exception of the various injuries and having to take the insurance day, everything more or less happened right on schedule. As any director will tell you, that's not always the case. Most directors are always prepared for something—anything—to go wrong. But things ran pretty smoothly on the *Superbad* set.

From day one, improvising was a constant element. Even though the script is pretty close to what you see in the final product, the actors were given wiggle room to hone their characters. The improvs weren't there to change the film's direction but to enhance the comedy and make it feel that much more authentic. When an audience member can't tell what's improv and what isn't, then you know it's not just gratuitous ad-libbing for ad-libbing's sake. It serves a purpose to the story, and in turn manages to make the film better.

When you're working on a film that relies on being more or less "in the moment" as a result of the ad-libs, the only way to keep up with that momentum is to utilize multiple cameras. This is especially the case for scenes with a heavy amount of dialogue. This practice— referred to as the "three-camera setup"—is common in sitcoms, but most films are traditionally done with a single camera. *Superbad's* filmmakers definitely took the opportunity to use multiple cameras whenever possible. One such example is the soccer sequence. Given how much back-and-forth there was in this scene, it made sense to run multiple cameras to capture any ad-libs that could materialize.

"Judd's approach is really not that dissimilar to someone like John Cassavetes," says Mottola. "It's just the really funny comedy guru version of it. You're trying to capture a moment on film. And that's the way Cassavetes would work, with multiple cameras."[20]

It also can be intimidating for a newcomer to come into such an improv-heavy environment for the first time. It's akin to being thrown to a pack of hungry wolves if you don't know what you're doing. It's bound to be even more daunting when you're seventeen years old and you've never been in a film before, like Emma Stone was. Luckily, Stone had done some improv training back in Arizona. When she was eleven—before she eventually moved to Los Angeles at fifteen—she started doing improv with a troupe at a local youth theater and fell in love with the format. But once she moved out to Los Angeles, she became more focused on going on auditions and didn't have a chance to do much else with improv. *Superbad* gave her that chance again.

Entering a new environment can be nerve-racking for any performer. But because so many people on *Superbad* had worked on other projects together, there was a built-in sense of camaraderie before cameras even started rolling. Only a handful of people on set were just entering the bubble for the first time. Emma Stone and Martha MacIsaac—both of whom were newcomers to working on an American studio comedy—quickly formed a bond. Stone also managed to form a close bond with Jonah Hill. If their chemistry onscreen looks authentic, that's because it was.

Perhaps one of the biggest scenes between Seth and Jules is the infamous home economics scene. After Seth's partner doesn't show up, he convinces the teacher to pair him up with Jules for the day. While Jules is diligently making their tiramisu, Seth is behind her back, doing every sort of obscene and perverse sexual gesture that he can think of. Like so much else, the scene—minus the sexual gestures, presumably—was based on another actual experience of Rogen's.

"I was finally partnered with a girl that I had a huge crush on for years and years and years and years," Rogen would later recount. "And it just seemed like the most organic conversation. It kind of felt like you were on a date every class in a weird way. Like 'We're cooking together!' It was like domestic role-play in a weird way. And then she dated me for two days and then dumped me."[21]

While Hill and Cera managed to strike up a bond prior to making the film, it only got stronger during production. There was a lot riding on the two being believable as friends on camera; luckily, they became friends in real life. That energy extended to the set. As Cera would later recall, "We just laugh all the time. I feel like I'm ten times funnier just by him being in the room. And life just feels ten times more fun."[22]

Speaking of laughing, Hill was on a mission to try and make Cera break character and laugh during a take. Throughout the entire shoot, however, he could never manage to do it. It wasn't until toward the end of production when, during a scene, Hill sneezed. For whatever reason, that's what finally did the trick.

The overall vibe was incredibly laid back on set. Shauna Robertson attributes this to the fact that Mottola was such a fine director who knew exactly what he wanted in advance. Perhaps the fact that there was already an intense familiarity between the cast and crew only made things easier. Because of this, many nights turned into post-shooting hang sessions. The filmmakers went out of their way to make the set a really fun place to be, reminiscent of how it would be if you were all suddenly back in high school. "They were so welcoming," Aviva Baumann remembers. "It felt like I was hanging out with my high school friends. They'd have parties, they'd invite people over. They were just incredibly kind and inclusive and hilarious. So we all clicked immediately. It showed in the film, too."[23]

Mottola adds, "I think when you're doing a movie with that many really funny people, it is extraordinarily funny. People are laughing all day long. So that in and of itself relaxes people. And I did not discourage it. I can't feel like I can take too much credit because the chemistry of that group of people was so great."[24]

Any high school movie is reliant on extras. When you shoot a scene in a school hallway, you're going to need access to a crowd of people to fill out the scene. Shooting these scenes can often be tricky to navigate. Because *Superbad* also has two house party scenes, shots at bars, and other big locations, they'd need as many hands on deck as possible. Most extras were cast the traditional way, but there were also reporters doing on-set visits that wound up in the film. Beyond that, the filmmakers also called upon some of their friends to come hang with them for the day for the crowd scenes.

When Seth and Evan go to the adult party with Francis, eagle-eyed comedy fans can spot a lot of noticeable faces, including Danny McBride, Ben Best, and Jody Hill. This is because everyone working on *Superbad* became huge fans of the film *The Foot Fist Way*, and they plucked the cast of the film to show up as extras in a scene. Also, just as importantly, they wanted to party with them. Robertson later recalled, "We just asked people to come hang out. We're like 'We can't pay anyone, but you can come hang out with us. And please will you just do a little part.' And it made it feel like we were all in high school so it was fun staying up until five in the morning with all your buddies."[25]

That party scene was reflective of the one that Rogen and Goldberg were at when they were fourteen. While the pig that bit Evan's foot never made it into the script, it does feature Evan accidentally winding up in a room with a group of guys—including David Krumholtz and Martin Starr—doing a bunch of coke. To help offset the awkwardness of the situation, Evan starts singing the song "These Eyes" by the Guess Who. Mottola later said about the scene, "It's a stretch to believe that a present day teen would know 'These Eyes,' but those songs don't go away. Classic rock never goes away. You can't walk into a deli without hearing one of those songs."[26]

They actually considered several different versions of that scene. One version had Evan singing "The Thong Song." Another alternative to the scene featured Evan freestyle rapping, while one was just an extended take of him dancing. At the time, Cera was really hopeful that "The Thong Song" would make the final cut. Alas, they wound up going with "These Eyes," which Cera eventually concluded was the right choice.[27]

Anytime you make a movie, there are certain legal requirements in place to ensure safety. One such requirement pertains to drinking on camera. For obvious reasons, the party scenes didn't actually feature people drinking alcohol. Instead, they used water to emulate vodka, apple juice for hard liquor, and other types of nonalcoholic beer. Imagine having to do take after take while actually drinking— that would make things pretty difficult the further along you got.

While the party sequence features some noticeable faces, the film isn't as cameo heavy as a lot of other Rogen and Apatow films are. Everything feels a lot more contained within the film. Still, some are sprinkled throughout. Two Fogell auditionees—Clark Duke and Dave Franco—have small parts in the film. Additionally, *Undeclared* alum Carla Gallo—who plays the character who bleeds on Seth's pants—and *Freaks and Geeks* alum Steve Bannos—who once again plays a math teacher—wind up in the film. There is another notable cameo in the film, though, one that even diehard movie fans might miss: Rogen's father. While Rogen's mom is responsible for the scene with the cops busting in on Fogell as he's losing his virginity, his dad actually manages to make his way into the film, playing the angry homeowner who throws a baseball bat at Seth as he's running through his backyard.

For Mintz-Plasse, the party atmosphere was interrupted by school. That's because at the time of filming, he was seventeen years old and the only minor on set. As a result, he wasn't able to enjoy the hang between takes as much as his counterparts did. While he was in algebra class, for instance, he would look out the window and see the cast going into the dailies trailer to hang out and watch footage during lunch breaks.

His age also prohibited him from being able to shoot late into the night. The solution was to shoot all of his night scenes in the car with the police officers in front of a green screen on a soundstage with LED rear-projection lights. When they would shoot on the street, they'd typically utilize a body double for Mintz-Plasse. During the car scenes, the body double—who obviously wasn't an actor—would just sit there awkwardly while Rogen and Hader essentially improvised *at* him.

Just as important as getting the chemistry right between Seth and Evan was the chemistry between Fogell and the two cops. This dynamic makes up 85 percent of Fogell's scenes—and 100 percent of the cop scenes. So it was crucial to make sure that chemistry showed on the film. Luckily, it did. As Hader would later recall about sharing scenes with Mintz-Plasse, "Working with him was great. He broke his wrist trick-or-treating. I went 'What happened?' He went 'Oh man. I was trick-or-treating with my homies. I fell and broke my wrist.' He was so cool that by the end of it I was like 'Oh, I should still be trick-or-treating.' He was such a confident performer and laid back. You felt while we were shooting that 'Oh man. This guy is gonna really pop in this movie.'"[28]

As Mintz-Plasse would recount, "For me, the number-one priority in comedy is feeling comfortable, because you want to feel safe. You don't want to feel like, if you say a bad joke, you're gonna get judged. With them, it's the complete opposite. They made me feel super comfortable to say whatever I wanted to say, however dumb it was or however wrong it was."[29]

The chemistry that Mintz-Plasse shared with Hader and Rogen translates to the screen. Most remarkably, it doesn't feel like the two cops are ever looking down on Fogell throughout the film, as they do with the other high schoolers in the movie. As obnoxious as the characters might be—not to mention unbelievably bad at their jobs—they have a certain paternal fondness as well as respect for Fogell. We watch as they take him under their wings.

Perhaps the most "epic" scene in the film features the two officers and Fogell lighting the police car on fire and then shooting guns at it. It was actually the first time Hader had shot a gun on camera, something he would become a lot more familiar with years later when he played the eponymous serial killer in HBO's *Barry*. To help prepare for shooting a gun on camera, Hader, Rogen, and Mintz-Plasse decided to go to a shooting range. It became a group outing. Cera and Hill wound up tagging along, although Hill apparently refused to go in, telling Hader, "Fuck that. No way I'm going in there." Hader also found himself uncomfortable with the idea of having people with live ammo shooting guns right next to him. He spent a lot of his time at the gun range smoking cigarettes outside with Hill. Everyone else had fun, though.[30]

At a certain point, their time at the shooting range became less about trying to train Mintz-Plasse with the type of gun he'd be shooting on camera—your standard handgun—and more about finding the biggest gun possible for him to shoot, which turned out to be a shotgun. Given how little he weighed at that point in time, the blast from the gun would literally throw him backward, and everyone would have to get out of the way. Mintz-Plasse would later reflect, "I weighed like 105 pounds. I'm the size of the shotgun. And I'm holding this thing and I shoot it and it like launches my whole body back. And I remember being like 'That was crazy.' And I'm turning the gun around, and everyone's like 'Fucking point it away, bro.' I had no idea what I was doing."[31]

The scene in the final film where the car is set on fire and Mintz-Plasse fires the gun is made even more epic thanks to the song choice. While filming the scene, Hader improvised by singing the song "Panama" by Van Halen. The choice is a stark contrast to the rest of the film's funky musical vibe, but in the scene, it fits. Immediately after the take, Apatow went over to Hader and let him know that the ad-lib just cost them a ton of money, as they now had to license the song.

Speaking of Hader, this was one scene he did not enjoy shooting. The script required him to do donuts in a parking lot in a car whose windshield is full of cracks. He had to lean his body out of the car just to be able to see. There were giant light poles in the parking lot, and every time he spun around, he was afraid that he was going to hit one. Mercifully, they completed the scene without incident.[32]

One of the film's biggest emotional moments is the sleeping bag scene. After both Seth and Evan have a rough night at the party—and both are very much still intoxicated—they end up in

Evan's basement, tucked into sleeping bags. What follows is the film's most earnest and authentic discussion about their friend- ship. By the end of the scene, they declare how much they love each other before going to sleep. It's this scene that really drives home what the movie is all about. It was never about the party or the alcohol or getting girls. It is about separation anxiety between two childhood best friends. Both Hill and Cera nail the scene, making you care about these two characters more than you ever expected to.

The scene was actually a late addition to the film. According to Mottola, Apatow felt like something was missing toward the end. There needed to be one more emotional beat before Evan and Seth go to the mall in the morning. What Rogen and Goldberg came up with was the sleeping bag scene, right before production was set to start. It turned out to be exactly what the film was missing. On the day of the shoot, Hill even improvised the moment where he "boops" Evan's nose in a hilariously sweet—albeit clearly drunken—manner.[33]

For the film's true final scene, Seth and Evan casually run into Jules and Becca at the mall the day after the party. In the sober light of day, there is some initial awkwardness that quickly goes away. For the first time, Seth and Evan are making an honest attempt at forging a connection with their crushes, realizing that they don't need a big party in order to make an impression. Nothing seems forced within this meet-cute. It's an idea that Apatow suggested and that Goldberg was initially hesitant to. He declared it as corny and "the lamest idea in the world."

Goldberg continued, "But when we had the actors there, I saw what Judd had been getting at the whole time. With the right actors there, you can make the right awkwardness so that this moment will be both a satisfying wrap-up and a not corny, tie-everything-to- gether kind of scene. Then Greg Mottola got the perfect music and the perfect shots with Russ Alsobrook. I don't know, they did it. I credit my lack of experience at the time with making me naive about how well that scene would have worked."[34]

As for the overall shoot, Mottola refers to it as being a "once-in-a-lifetime" experience. With all of the challenges that the creative team had to conquer just to get to the point where they were on the set, it's remarkable that the film got greenlit at all. For years, Rogen and Goldberg were repeatedly told *no* when it came to *Superbad*. Now, not only were they told *yes*, but they got to do it on their own terms. And on these terms, everyone was able to enjoy themselves while getting to make the movie. As Apatow recalls, "Seth and Evan had done such detailed, obsessive work on the script over many years that by the time we got to the shoot, it was almost like a play that had been tried out of town."[35]

There was already an indication that they had something special on their hands at this point. Robertson would later remember the vibe when watching the footage they shot the day before, called dailies, during lunch, which is a common practice on any film. As they watched *Superbad* dailies, they'd find themselves laughing. They figured that if it was making them laugh, perhaps audiences would have the same reaction. Only time would tell how truthful that would be.[36]

The film also wasn't backing down in regard to going all the way to the edge. It would have been a shame if Rogen and Goldberg's script, containing everything that they wanted to see in the ultimate high school movie, would go too soft at the zero hour. In fact, not only are the raunchy scenes some of the film's most memorable, but they also remain among the most challenging.

9

Drawings and Stains

When you think about the scenes that pushed the envelope in regards to what they could get away with, a few in particular come to mind. Yes, it could be argued that the film is littered with boundary-pushing comedic moments—all of which somehow manage to land. But it's these specific moments that the filmmakers were definitely expecting some pushback on. They fought to make sure that what we see on the screen is exactly what Rogen and Goldberg had intended years earlier.

When Seth and Evan go to the adult party, Seth winds up dancing with a drunk girl, played by Carla Gallo. After they're done, a fellow partygoer points out to Seth that he's got a stain on his pants. It's revealed that the drunk girl was on her period, and the stain on his pants is blood. This immediately leads to a near-brawl with her boyfriend, who has a similar stain on his pants. Like so much else in the film, this scene was based on a true story. However, it happened to a friend of theirs—not Rogen—while at a high school dance. In the locker room after the dance, Rogen and Goldberg noticed a stain on one of their friends' pants. They were all trying to deduce how it got there. One scenario that played through their heads was that maybe someone had spilled wine on his leg at some point. Then, they noticed another group of high schoolers on the other side of the locker room having the exact same conversation. That's when it dawned on everyone that it was blood.

It's the sort of moment you can't possibly make up, one of those things that has to have happened in real life. How do you not put it in the script? It fit the film like a glove. Still, there was some debate within the studio and among the film's creatives regarding whether or not they could get away with actually shooting it. Even Mottola had his own initial reservations on whether or not that scene would work.

"I am enough of a lapsed Catholic that, when I first read it, I was like *Oh. Is that offensive to women?*" Mottola recalls asking himself at the time. "I really did think about it. I didn't want to do something that crossed the wrong line. The thing that sold it is they told me it's a true story. And I thought, *You know what? If it's a true story, this isn't some writer making something up to shock for the sake of shock. If it happened, that's good by me.*"[1]

The filmmakers were most likely expecting a brawl with the studio over the joke similar to the one in the film. Indeed, there were some long discussions behind the scenes. One of the biggest issues is that once Seth's got the stain on his pants, it has to stay there for the entirety of the movie. Unless they're going to spend the money to digitally remove the stain in postproduction, they'd be stuck with it. As Apatow recalls, "It was always one of those ideas where we thought, *This is an all or nothing type of joke idea. It's either going to be really funny and people are going to get it or they're going to be horrified and it's going to sink the movie.*"[2]

As for the studio, they reacted with a little bit of fear. Some had concerns over whether or not the scene was even funny. Amy Pascal didn't care about any reservations some may have had and didn't pay any attention to it. As far as she was concerned, it was funny. The studio, however, wanted to make sure they got enough coverage so that they could cut around it in case the scene didn't work with test audiences and they had to remove it. The filmmakers talked about potential ways that they could explain the stain if its origin had to be cut, like having Seth spilling a drink on his pants at the party.

"The truth is, it would've been difficult to take out," says Mottola. "I think we pretended like we had enough coverage to get around it. But really, we were like, 'This better work because I don't know how we're going to get rid of that stain on Jonah's pants for the rest of the movie.' I remember when the on-set painter was painting the stain on his pants, and I was like 'Bigger. Nope, bigger.' They were like 'Really?' 'Nope. Bigger. Keep going. We've got to see that.' They were like 'This is big enough.' 'Nope. Make it bigger. If we're going to do it, we're going to do it.'"[3]

As soon as Mottola rehearsed the scene with Hill, he became convinced that it would work. Even if the studio were to object once they saw the film, there was little that could be done outside of removing it with CGI, which would far exceed the $20 million they spent to make the movie. They backed themselves into a corner with the stain. It was in.

The infamous penis-drawing sequence also required an intense amount of deliberation. While it is now a staple of the film and one of the first things you might think about when someone mentions *Superbad*, a lot of painstaking preparation went into bringing that idea to the big screen.

In the film, the character of Seth admits to Evan that he had been obsessed with drawing pictures of dicks when he was a young kid. The film then shows a flashback to all of Seth's penis drawings. One fateful day, however, Seth drops one of his drawings in class, and Evan's future crush Becca picks it up and is traumatized. She reports the drawing to the principal, which gets Seth in all sorts of trouble. He even has to stop eating penis-shaped food. Seth laments to Evan, "Do you know how many foods are shaped like dicks? The best kinds!"

This idea also has an element of truth to it, but not what you'd expect. Growing up, Evan Goldberg also liked to draw. Not dicks, however, as he was very quick to point out. He was self-conscious about his drawings, never thinking they were any good. So when he'd draw, he'd cover them with his hand. He and Rogen incorporated this into the script as a reason for Becca to dislike Seth. The two writers started brainstorming what the craziest possible thing a character could be drawing as a child, and the answer was ostensibly crazy pictures of penises.[4]

It should go without saying that there are certain things that you cannot legally have around young, impressionable children. Just because you're making a movie that exists in a fictional world doesn't mean that all laws are thrown out the window during production. So, naturally, the penis drawings instigated a legal discussion. Apatow would later recall literally being in a room with four or five different lawyers, talking about the California child labor laws and what the kids could and could not see. As Tolmach remembers, "I was in—I can't tell you how many—meetings with the lawyer and the filmmakers to try to figure out how that actually got done."[5]

The irony of that legal discussion is that the penises you see in the movie ended up being drawn by a future lawyer: Goldberg's brother, David, who was in Canada studying for law school. David drew literally hundreds of penises that wound up in the film. At one point, a group led by Mottola were huddled in an office with no less than fifty penis drawings sprawled out on the floor, having a serious discussion about which ones would go in the movie. So much thought— and debate—went into the film's silliest gag. But there was a delicate tightrope they all had to walk.

The next hurdle became how to shoot the scene without the children actually seeing what was going on. They had to storyboard every moment within an inch of its life. An adult female crew member actually held the penis drawings you see in the film. The young Seth and Becca characters never actually see the drawings, thus avoiding a potential legal fiasco. There was so much scrutiny over the drawings, in fact, that they were kept under lock and key to avoid them leaking out to some of the minor actors. The drawings were literally kept in envelopes until it was time to shoot the inserts.

Young Seth was played by a ten-year-old actor named Casey Margolis, who later said about the scene, "I don't think I really understood what was going on. My parents did, they read the script. I didn't really read the script. I just kind of did what I was told."[6]

Playing Becca was Laura Marano, who was eleven years old at the time and would later go on to star in the Disney Channel series *Austin & Ally*, as well as many other film and TV projects. Unlike Margolis, she had read the script beforehand. Once she did, she can only describe feeling "horrified." When directing the scene, Mottola told her that she was looking at a paper depicting two guys fighting, but she knew the truth. When she did finally see the film many years later, she wound up loving it and embracing how funny it was.[7]

Despite the headaches they had to go through to get to what you see in the film, the montage actually became Mottola's favorite thing to shoot. After principal photography wrapped, Mottola went to the set of *Pineapple Express*, deep in the woods, to shoot all the close-ups of the dick drawings. There were literally hundreds of penis drawings created for the film, each of them having its own distinctive look. One drawing featured a penis riding a missile à la *Dr. Strangelove*. Another featured a penis with pigtails resembling the Wendy's girl. Another drawing was a very erect George Washington. If there was a way to add a penis to something, the filmmakers had it covered.

With Mintz-Plasse still technically a minor during production, the filmmakers had to dance around potential legal issues relating to him as well. (Though one imagines he was in the clear to look at the penis drawings.) There was no scene more challenging to shoot with Fogell than the sex scene between him and his love interest, Nicola. At the time, Mintz-Plasse had never even really kissed a girl. So his reaction was essentially "Oh my God. I'm going to shoot a sex scene? That's crazy."[8]

The only issue was that Mintz-Plasse couldn't actually be on top of his costar, who was a few years older than him. In the original script, Nicola was supposed to be naked in the scene. However, Aviva Baumann approached the filmmakers and told them that, as much as she loved the script, she wasn't comfortable shooting a nude scene because her grandma would watch it. Luckily, the filmmakers had no problem with forgoing the nudity.

Mottola recalls how they decided to shoot the scene to avoid any legal issues: "I thought, *The way I'm going to do this is close-ups, so basically the camera is her point of view then it flips and the camera becomes his point of view.* So that they would never have to be on top of each other very much. We'd do a wide shot to get her into position on top of him, but we wouldn't spend an enormous amount of potentially illegal time with both of them uncomfortably faking sex."[9]

The studio was insistent that there couldn't be any sort of grinding. After it was shot, the studio watched the scene repeatedly to ensure that there wasn't anything illegal or questionable in it. The resulting scene instead shows Fogell exclaiming, "Oh my god, it's in," before Hader's character immediately comes in to interrupt him. But because Mintz-Plasse was underage, that also meant that he legally had to have a guardian on set with him when the scene was shot. That guardian was his mom. As Mintz-Plasse recalls, "She had to come down [to the set], which was pretty uncomfortable. She was loving it up. She was having the time of her life, watching her son do that."[10]

Adds Baumann, "It was so funny because everybody was normally laughing and loud and excited. In that scene, all of the guys were dead silent. I couldn't get eye contact from anyone. I walked up like 'Okay, what are we doing?' And everybody just got so shy and awkward."[11]

Despite the awkwardness from everyone on set, the scene got done. When it came time for the cops to walk in on Fogell and Nicola, it required about thirty-five takes. This is because everyone—particularly Hader—couldn't stop laughing. It got so bad that Mottola eventually pulled Hader aside and told him, "Maybe you need to go take a walk."[12]

Fogell was not the only character who had to film an awkward sexual scene. Ironically, though, he is the only character in the film that actually winds up having sex, albeit ever so briefly. While Seth is perhaps the one who is the most certain that this is the night that he and Evan are finally going to have sex with their crushes, he also manages, in a hilarious twist of fate, to strike out the worst. When he goes to kiss Jules, she rejects him because he's drunk. When she tries to comfort him, he winds up accidentally headbutting her when he passes out.

To prepare for the scene, Hill actually got himself blackout drunk. This proved to be an issue later on, as Hill had a second scene to shoot that night where his character isn't drunk. So there's a scene in the film where Hill is trying to hide his inebriation as best he can. Thankfully, it's never too noticeable in the final cut, and this marked the only time on set that Hill was actually drunk.[13]

Cera's character also has an awkward sexual encounter of his own. He finds himself in a bedroom and is just about to consummate with his love interest, Becca. Everything is going according to how he built it up in his head, except for the fact that he never expected her to be as intoxicated as she is. Finally, he follows his moral compass and admits to himself that Becca is far too drunk. Once he lets her know that he's uncomfortable and doesn't want to go through with it, she throws up all over the bed.

The nerves of filming such an awkward scene got the best of the performers here. MacIsaac had a mimosa before she shot her very first drunk scene, just to help boost her confidence. Cera was also drunk during the scene, which helped take the pressure off both actors. Acting drunk on film is definitely strange, because you need to be believable—there's a fine line between being believably drunk and completely overdoing it. It's definitely uncomfortable, especially if you've never done it before. The fact that both performers had drank before their big scene took away some of that awkwardness.[14]

The scene features a lot of the uncomfortable dirty talk that was present in MacIsaac's audition. Most comically, MacIsaac improvised when her character told Evan that she was going to give him "the best blowjay ever." An earlier version of the script managed to get even filthier. One of Becca's lines was telling Evan to "lick my hairy love crack." MacIsaac actually had to read this line during her audition, and she remained hopeful it would be cut. By the time she finally said it during a take, the crew immediately agreed, and Goldberg told her they were cutting the line.[15]

MacIsaac was definitely nervous before shooting the bedroom scene, even with the help of liquid courage. Luckily it came toward the end of the shoot, which turned out to be smart scheduling because it allowed Cera and MacIsaac enough time to have gotten to know each other throughout the filming. But it was still awkward, and not for the reasons you'd think: even though Cera wasn't a minor and didn't need to have supervision, his mom actually brought him to work that day. That made MacIsaac more uncomfortable given the nature of the scene and what Cera's mom would have to see her do to her son. Luckily, his mom left pretty quickly.

With all the scenes shot—even the most difficult ones—everybody could breathe a sigh of relief. The film was in the can after a forty-two-day shoot. This allowed the actors to move on to their next projects. Or in the case of Mintz-Plasse, it meant finishing out high school. "It never felt real," he later said. "I thought the movie would come out and make a couple bucks than go away. I had no idea what could happen."[16]

What would wind up happening would far exceed anyone's expectations. If nothing else, the entire cast and crew could be proud that they got through production, making the movie they set out to. The fact that they had so much fun doing it was only icing on the cake.

10

Testing It Out

While many film shoots utilize improv to find one or two additional beats that improve the script, in the case of *Superbad*, it was more than just those one or two beats. Practically every scene gave the editor an array of different options to choose from.

Bill Kerr was enlisted as the film's editor. Like so many other people involved in *Superbad*, he had a familiar relationship with the filmmakers, as he had served as the editor on *Undeclared*. He also had experience working on such comedy films as *Tommy Boy*, *Along Came Polly*, *Undercover Brother*, and *Nutty Professor II: The Klumps*. As Mottola recalls about editing with Kerr, "By and large, that was a great collaboration. Bill's really smart and has a great sense of timing and tempo."[1]

Having a director and an editor who are in sync is imperative to the editing process. The last thing you'll want to have is disagreements in the editing room. This has caused some productions to come to a standstill or go off the rails entirely, leading to a director or editor that is unhappy with the final product. Luckily, that wasn't the case here. Mottola says that he and Kerr agreed on "most things." There were a few places, however, where Kerr wanted to go for more of a broader comedy feel than what Mottola was looking for. But there were never any big disagreements about it.[2]

Mottola's goal in editing remained the same as it had always been throughout the making of the film—to keep it as grounded as possible in realism. Even the over-the-top police officers, who are played to be ridiculous, are not shot that way. Their sequences were always shot as if they were in a drama, not a comedy. It's the script that informs the humor. For experimenting purposes, Mottola had asked for an Avid—a pre-laptop editing system that was predominant in the industry—in his office, just so he could play around with different things for the film. He doesn't think he ever came up with anything that was better than what Kerr came up with, though. More than anything else, this was just a way for Mottola to look through dailies so he didn't have to keep bothering Kerr all the time to show him stuff.

"We didn't cut many scenes," Mottola said in an interview at the time. "We would just swap out different jokes or different moments. Or we would find versions of scenes that were a little more broad or try something that was a little more subtle."[3]

After finally settling on the tone of the film, it was time to show the rough cut to Rogen, Goldberg, and Apatow. Mottola found it painful to show the film at this point, as he still felt it was too long. Nevertheless, it was ultimately a successful process, as he managed to get some great notes from the rest of the team. From there, he ultimately had a better sense of what could be cut. One thing that Mottola felt strongly about, though, was the penis drawing scene.

Mottola says, "That was one thing Bill Kerr wanted to cut. When the film was too long, he said 'We don't need this flashback. It doesn't move the story forward at all.' And I said 'Yeah, we have to have the flashback.' It's part of what makes the movie what it is. Sometimes it doesn't need to move the story forward. Sometimes it just needs to be funny."[4]

While the filmmakers eventually nixed the idea of doing TV-safe lines during production, the film still had to have the actors come back in to do ADR, which stands for automated dialogue replacement. This is a common practice in the industry where the actors will head into the studio and rerecord some of their lines. Often a technical issue will crop up, such as background noise interfering with the dialogue. Actors also rerecord unsuitable dialogue for TV, such as curse words. *Superbad* had a *lot* of unsuitable dialogue.

Normally, it's a pretty tedious process. A lot of actors struggle to get the new line readings to match up with what their lips are saying onscreen. But not Bill Hader. As Mottola recalls, Hader's were some of his favorite contributions, not to mention some of the funniest alternate lines he'd ever heard. For example, instead of shouting "Jesus Christ," Hader would yell "John Cheever." "J. D. Salinger" also got thrown in there from time to time. He'd just keep shouting out classic author's names. Sadly, none made it into the final TV cut.[5]

For the film's opening sequence, Mottola found inspiration in the '70s classic *Foxy Brown*. He wanted to have Hill and Cera dancing in front of a green screen for the opening credits. It's a sequence that he worked on with the titles editor, Scott Davids, and it really does a good job of setting the tone, as does utilizing the 1970s-era Columbia logo. As for the end credits, they realized they had an abundance of penis drawings that didn't make the final cut. Their solution was to feature them throughout the end credits.

At one point, Evan Goldberg had an idea for Michael Cera to keep dancing on camera for the DVD menu. According to Cera, he told him, "We can have a DVD menu that the menu screen will be an hour long, and it won't loop. So I want you to dance for an hour, so that somebody will watch the DVD menu waiting for it to loop, but it never will for an hour." So Cera shot some more footage by himself that was solely to be used for the DVD menu.[6]

A film's soundtrack helps set the entire tone. *Superbad*'s music supervisor was Jonathan Karp, who had worked on a variety of comedy films and television shows starting in the 1990s, including *Zoolander*, *Punch-Drunk Love*, *Starsky & Hutch*, and, yes, with Apatow on *Freaks and Geeks*, *The 40 Year-Old Virgin*, and *Knocked Up*. It was on the latter that he first learned about *Superbad*.

Music rights are a big deal in the film and TV world. The more sought after a song is, the more money it's going to cost to put it in the film. You have to be very strategic about just how far you can stretch your music budget. A lot of times, it comes down to just how badly you need a specific song in a specific scene. When they approached Van Halen about putting "Panama" in the film, they wanted half a million dollars for it. For a film that only had a $20 million budget, that would've eaten up a chunk of it; the entire music budget would've been blown by that one song. Luckily, the marketing team was already cutting the song into trailers and the film's marketing materials. This gave Mottola an idea: he got approval for the licensing fee to come out of the marketing budget instead of the film budget.[7]

One thing that Karp made sure of was that each character had his or her own distinctive musical vibe. A lot of the scenes with the three leads feature funk and R&B tunes. When the cops are onscreen, they have more of a classic rock vibe. For the adult party, Karp uses what he calls "dirtbag" type music. Then at Jules's party, the music is more contemporary, featuring modern hip-hop tracks. These genres can be interchangeable depending on the circumstance, but for the most part, the music cues make sense for each character.

The soundtrack itself is stacked with big names, practically an embarrassment of musical riches: the Bar-Kays, Jean Knight, Curtis Mayfield, the Roots, Rick James, Sergio Mendes & Brasil '66, Ted Nugent, the Guess Who, the Remains, the Coup, Motörhead, KC and the Sunshine Band, the Four Tops, the Notorious B.I.G., the Rapture, and the Amboy Dukes.

There's more to a film's soundtrack than just securing music from popular artists; there's large chunks that need to be scored. When you've got a film called *Superbad* and you're already playing into the '70s aesthetic, you'll need to ensure that the film's soundtrack follows suit. So the filmmakers brought on Lyle Workman. Just like every other department head, composer Workman was pulled from Apatow's rolodex of talent.

Workman had previously worked on *The 40 Year-Old Virgin*, as well as on the IFC series *Dinner for Five* and the Jon Favreau movie *Made*. Before that, Workman was sought after as a guitarist in the industry, having played on two Todd Rundgren albums, and was a session musician for artists such as Sting, Beck, Ziggy Marley, Norah Jones, Michael Bublé, Sheryl Crow, Shakira, and They Might Be Giants. Oddly enough, Workman also had experience playing in a funk band back in high school. He was perfect for the task at hand.

During Workman's meeting with Apatow, the producer told him that he had three projects in mind for him: *Knocked Up*, John C. Reilly's music biopic parody *Walk Hard*, and *Superbad*. Workman was initially drawn to *Knocked Up*, as Apatow was the director on that one. But they already had Loudon Wainwright III in mind for that film, and perhaps Workman could work alongside Wainwright on it. But they wanted him to tackle *Superbad* solo.

When Workman came on board, they already knew they wanted the film to have that funky tone. The title of *Superbad* suggested as much. Early on, Mottola had a conversation with Rogen about the music. He told him, "You've named this movie *Superbad*. What if we did an all-funk score? What if we harken back to sort of the slightly freewheeling sense of fun and slight subversiveness of those movies with the soundtrack?" Rogen was into the genius idea of juxtaposing a cool soundtrack with three nerdy white guys running around trying to get alcohol, so that's what they did.[8]

Workman recalls, "A lot of times for composers, it's a clean slate when they start a movie. So it's like 'What am I going to do??' But this was very set. So credit to them for coming up with such a great idea. For me, it was just making sure that it was authentic. That was really in the writing and the casting of the musicians."[9]

Workman collaborated with local musicians to perfect a demo by the time they hired actual session musicians. When it came time to cast those musicians, they thought, why not bring in the guys who had actually worked on a lot of those James Brown songs? The name at the top of the list was Bootsy Collins. When Collins came on board, he suggested that they also seek out some of the other key components to that music, including Bernie Worrell and Catfish Collins (Bootsy's older brother), as well as two of James Brown's drummers, Clyde Stubblefield and Jabo Starks. Everyone said yes.

"It was just a pretty joyous and crazy couple of days," Karp recalls. "Most of those guys hadn't seen each other in years. The spirit in the studio was very much like a family reunion. They were just so happy to see each other and spend this time in each other's company, in addition to the excitement about playing on the score and the music that Lyle had created. That was just an incredible thing to witness and be a part of."[10]

Collins said in an interview during the recording sessions, "I talked to Lyle, and he wanted me to play bass with him on the soundtrack. So I suggested that if he was doing something that was called *Superbad*—I didn't even know what the movie was—but if it's called *Superbad*, then you need to get the 'Super Bad' cats to do it. I was really glad about it, because it gave us all a chance to get back together as a unit."[11]

Typically, a session like this would be done in a single day, even if you were dealing with an orchestral score that required thirty to forty minutes of music. *Superbad* only required fifteen, but they had set aside four days to get it done at Capitol Records in Los Angeles. That's because they had to do a lot of rehearsing, as not everything was learned in advance. For Workman, not only did he want the style of the music to be authentically '70s, but he also wanted to avoid any modern gear to make it.

Workman recalls, "I remember the woman who was representing both drummers. When we got into the details, one detail was 'Well, they would like to have these newer, modern kits to rent for the sessions.' And I asked them 'Can we please use old kits?' I live in Los Angeles, so the ability to rent drums from the '60s and the '70s is a no-brainer. And they agreed. So I wanted to make sure that everyone was playing the right kind of gear."[12]

Everything went smoothly during the four days of recording, and they got everything they needed out of it. Going into the sessions, Workman knew that he wasn't just going to record thirty-second cues instead of full songs like you typically would. Instead, he composed full-length tracks so they could run longer on the soundtrack. At long last, *Superbad* had found its rhythm.

When you're dealing with any type of comedy, the audience's reaction is the most crucial element. If your audience isn't laughing, what you've made isn't funny, and therefore it isn't technically successful. This sort of temperature check doesn't happen with most other genres—for example, unless you've got tears running down your cheeks and you're obnoxiously weeping loudly enough for everyone around you to hear, it's hard to register just how much you like a dramatic film. But with a comedy, laughter says everything, and *Superbad* needed to have the audience laughing from start to finish—except for when they were crying at the end of the film.

That's why test screenings are especially important when you're dealing with a comedy. While nobody likes having their art critiqued by an audience composed of random strangers, it's all part of the process. You have to do a certain number of test screenings so the studio can gauge the reaction, but you'll also find out if you have to make more cuts to your film.

Test screenings are also tedious, generating lots of notes for the filmmakers about changes they can make. Some creatives—if not most—view it as a necessary chore to tell you what you're doing right. So no one went in with any idea of what to expect, particularly with a movie as dirty as *Superbad* is. In fact, the filmmakers were so unsure of how it would go that they told Hill and Cera they couldn't attend in the event the audience had hated them. Fortunately, the audience had the opposite reaction during that first test screening.

"I thought that when we showed *Superbad* to audiences, we would start an ongoing debate about how dirty should the movie be," Apatow recalled. "And at the very first screening, nobody in the audience had any issue with anything in the movie in the numbers that would make you change it. I couldn't believe it. I thought we would be debating so many set pieces and language and cutting things. And there was nothing."[13]

Added Rogen about waiting to watch the bloodstain scene with a crowd for the first time, "I think that's the most nervous I've ever been in my life, at that first screening when the period-blood scene started. We would have had to reshoot something. I was horrified, absolutely horrified."[14]

From the first test screening—at the Avco Theater, which is no longer there—in front of what Mottola describes as a "youthful audience," everything went off like gangbusters. The movie couldn't have been received better. Apatow considers it maybe the best first test screening any of his films ever had. At the end of the screening, Mottola turned around to see two teenage girls crying because they were so moved by the tender final scenes with Seth and Evan. Not only did *Superbad* have the audience laughing, it even managed to tug on some heartstrings, too.[15, 16]

Hader went to the screening with director Edgar Wright and writer Michael Bacall and wound up sitting next to Emma Stone and her mom. Afterward, as they were walking out, Hader and Stone shared the excitement with each other, and just how crazy that first screening felt. As both were relatively new to the film world, it was unlike anything that either of them had gone through before.

Mottola recalls, "I was fully expecting *Okay, we're going to see reports. We're going to hear about numbers. We're going to talk about what needs to still change or we need to do reshoots.* Basically all the things that happen after you have a test screening. And instead, it was just like 'Okay. The movie's ready to go. Let's finish it up and send it out.' I can't say that I've ever had that experience since."[17]

The studio execs got more and more excited as the film progressed. They were able to see that the gamble was paying off. The laughs were so huge that lines were getting drowned out. People were immersed in this world. The film nobody wanted to make for all those years was finally paying off. Sony could tell it had a massive hit on its hands.

Despite the early positive response to the test screening, the film didn't seem to be building in public awareness. You can get a good sense of what sort of buzz there is for a specific film through its tracking numbers, which will give you a rough idea of how your film could open. The numbers weren't where the filmmakers wanted them to be. Apatow knew that if *Superbad* was going to open as big as he knew it could, they needed to spend more money on marketing. So he called up Sony president Amy Pascal.

"I remember jumping on a call with Amy Pascal begging her to throw more money into commercials," recalls Apatow, "because we all felt like when people discover this, it's going to take off. And she went for it. She spent—I think—another nine million dollars on marketing, and we released the first five minutes of the movie [online]. And that led to a really strong opening."[18]

Releasing the first five minutes of the film would serve as the perfect appetizer to get people hyped about the film. After the funky opening credits, we're immediately pulled into Seth and Evan's world, in which they discuss what type of porn they want to sign up for at college the next year. Right away this tells you what type of film it is. While it doesn't quite prepare you for the more tender moments, it serves as the perfect introduction to find out who these characters are.

The film continued to test through the roof. Famed director Cameron Crowe was an early admirer of *Superbad*. Apatow personally invited him to a test screening because he was someone who had inspired everyone who worked on the film, thanks to *Fast Times at Ridgemont High*. Not only was it the first film Crowe ever wrote, but it is also a seminal 1980s high school film. It's a film that—like *Superbad*—takes a more realistic comedic approach to portraying high school, in stark contrast to the zany antics of a movie like *Porky's*. In *Fast Times* we see characters dealing with serious issues like abortion at a time when such topics were just not tackled in mainstream projects. Hill and Cera were especially freaking out after meeting Crowe, who said nice things to them about their performance.

All films have to be subjected to a rating by the Motion Picture Association, or MPA, which is notorious for taking a harsh stance when it comes to comedies, particularly in terms of vulgarity. There have been countless films that received an initial NC-17 rating whose filmmakers had to take them through the appeals process and advocate for an R rating instead. This was the case with *American Pie*, which had to cut a scene at a party to earn its R rating. With *Superbad*, however, nobody involved remembers there being a struggle or anything that they had to cut to get that R rating. When you really stop and think about how far the film pushes the envelope and does things that hadn't been done on film before, it's actually sort of shocking. This is something that Mottola says seems "miraculous in hindsight."[19]

After the incredible test screenings, the next step was to see how well it did with an actual fan base. Test screenings are one thing, but they're not necessarily made up of the target demographic. Many feature a more diverse audience to see how commercial a film might be. That July, *Superbad* was put to the ultimate test when Sony decided to bring the film—and its cast—to San Diego Comic Con. Once a "niche" event, the convention found itself getting more and more commercialized in the years leading up to 2007. At a certain point, Comic Con broadened its scope beyond comic books and embraced all things pop culture. It became the place where major film studios would go to trot out their latest projects and see how fans would respond. For film geeks, this is their empire. A project's reception there would immediately give everyone a sense of just how things would play out when the film would be released into the wild.

"The test screening had gone so well," Mottola says, "but it didn't quite prepare me for Comic Con, which has a level of enthusiasm that I've not seen since. It's kind of like a rock concert. People really, really get into it. It's kind of a beautiful reminder of the power of popular culture."[20]

On July 27, audiences were treated to the first-ever official screening of the film. It was followed by a Q and A with Greg Mottola, Judd Apatow, Seth Rogen, Michael Cera, Jonah Hill, Evan Goldberg, and Christopher Mintz-Plasse. You could not have asked for a better debut screening of a film. Although, realistically, the enthusiastic reaction should not have been a surprise to anyone involved. The film was already testing great, and at Comic Con, just like in the test screenings, entire lines of dialogue were being drowned out by the excessive laughter. After such a long journey to this point, it suddenly became clear to everyone that it was paying off.

As Tolmach recalls, "It just crushed. It was an incredibly smart thing to do. All of the marketing people were there, all of the production people were there. And you suddenly saw the movie of a generation happening, because you saw the way that people were reacting, and it was insane."[21]

Apatow adds, "I had never gone before. So to suddenly be in a room with five thousand fans doing a press conference was somewhat terrifying. I remember watching the movie and having it go over really well. The comic book fans could certainly relate to our leads, that's for sure."[22]

The following day, the film was presented as part of Sony's panel in the prestigious Hall H. This was hallowed ground at the convention center that weekend, and each studio selects their biggest tickets to parade around during the panel. The same group from the night before assembled in Hall H. Also joining the panel was Charlyne Yi, who was reportedly dating Cera at the time. Later, Yi admitted that the relationship was fictionalized for the 2009 film *Paper Heart*. As Mottola recalls, though, Edward Norton was also with the *Superbad* gang at Comic Con, which makes sense as he was dating Shauna Robertson, whom he would later marry. Because he was so recognizable, though, he opted to walk around the con floor in an Iron Man mask.[23]

Judging by the reaction the *Superbad* cast got, it was already clear that there was an undeniable excitement about the film. The stars were getting the full VIP treatment. Women were practically throwing themselves at Cera, giving him their hotel room numbers and asking to have his baby. Cera later shrugged it off and chalked it up to Comic Con being Comic Con. This was a month before the film was even released. This is based simply on a trailer and some clips. The raucous crowd hadn't seen anything yet.[24]

"It was really fun to see how hilarious Seth and Michael and Jonah and Bill Hader were in any situation where there were crowds and Q and As," Apatow recalls. "They were all amazing live performers, riotously funny on their feet. I almost compare it to The Beatles when they were really funny at those press conferences at airports. Nobody was burnt out. Nobody was over it. They got a big kick out of being with people and making them laugh and interacting with the fans."[25]

It's hard to imagine *Superbad* getting this type of reception had they premiered at a film festival. Sony knew that they had to bring the film to the core audience, and Comic Con was the place to find it. By the time the Con rolled around, promotion was in full swing. Everybody wanted to be surrounded by the cast of *Superbad*. Practically overnight, they were all entering the rock-star phase of their careers, even before the film came out. That's how strong the buzz had gotten, and they would find themselves riding similar waves all the way up to the premiere.

The reception at Comic Con only managed to get everyone at the studio even more excited. As great as the test screenings had gone, there was now this second wave, and everyone realized just what they had on their hands. As a result, the marketing team was now thinking of new and nontraditional ways that they could double down on the film.

11

The Publicity Rocket

Leading up to the premiere of *Superbad*, all signs were pointing to the film being a massive success. It had consistently tested through the roof, and everyone was still on that San Diego Comic Con high. Even more than that, the film would be following in the footsteps of another comedy blockbuster juggernaut, *Knocked Up*. It was about to become the summer of Seth Rogen.

Like *Superbad*, *Knocked Up* was already generating some major buzz prior to its early summer release. Given the success of *The 40 Year-Old Virgin* before it, a lot of people were speculating that the film could be the next big summer comedy. With the talent involved, hope was high for its success. If it did well, it could help pave the way to even more interest in *Superbad*.

In an interview with *Entertainment Weekly*, however, Rogen more or less deflected the notion that *Knocked Up* could be the next summer blockbuster. He pointed directly to the stiff competition of that summer's release schedule. They were trying to open a light-hearted comedy that follows a character realizing it's time to grow up when he unexpectedly gets a woman pregnant after a one-night stand against a staggering amount of tentpole films, remakes, and sequels: *Spider-Man 3, Transformers, Shrek the Third, Pirates of the Caribbean: At World's End, Harry Potter and the Order of the Phoenix, Fantastic Four: Rise of the Silver Surfer, Live Free or Die Hard, The Simpsons Movie, The Bourne Ultimatum, Halloween, Mr. Bean's*

Holiday, *Hairspray*, and *Rush Hour 3*. That's not even including stand-alone films like *Ratatouille*, *Surf's Up*, *Hot Rod*, and *I Now Pronounce You Chuck and Larry*. The work was cut out for them, and Rogen seemed to be aware of such.

"I don't think it's possible," Rogen said rather matter-of-factly about how *Knocked Up* in particular would thrive that summer. "There are too many other movies coming out. I mean, *Knocked Up*'s good, but we don't have, like, f—ing pirates and people swinging from webs. [Pregnant pause] We do have vagina shots, though. They don't have that. How many vaginas are there in *Shrek 3*? None that I know of."[1]

It wasn't crazy to be feeling a bit of pressure when you analyze what they were actually up against in 2007. Both *Knocked Up* and *Superbad* were coming out in the midst of one of the highest-grossing summers in cinema history, bringing in a then-record-breaking $4 billion at the box office, all within the span of four months. This was quite a feat—everybody ended up spending their entire summer going to the movies.

Despite the competition, Rogen was proven wrong when *Knocked Up* managed to hold its own in theaters. Once again, the notion that audiences were hungry for more raunchy comedies was proven accurate. Critically, the film was a smash hit, generating 89 percent "Fresh" reviews according to Rotten Tomatoes. The general consensus reads that the film is "a hilarious, poignant and refreshing look at the rigors of courtship and child-rearing, with a sometimes raunchy, yet savvy script that is ably acted and directed." At the end of the year, it even wound up on several critics top ten lists, including the *New York Post*, *LA Weekly*, *A.V. Club*, *Newsweek*, *Rolling Stone*, and the *New York Times*.[2]

The film wasn't just a critical hit, either. It was also a huge commercial success for Universal. It debuted at number two at the box office and managed to bring in a worldwide gross of nearly

$200 million. Factor in that it had just a $25 million budget and starred someone who was just about to break out but hadn't yet and you'll realize just how big of a deal that was. The Apatow camp was definitely celebrating this victory. But they also knew there was potentially more on the horizon.

If nothing else, this could only get everyone even more excited for the prospects of *Superbad*. Yes, *The 40 Year-Old Virgin* brought in over $100 million, but that was also two years earlier and things change rapidly in the industry. Just because a formula works in 2005 doesn't mean that formula will be met with the same response in 2007. To have a like-minded film doing so well—particularly one made by the same people who made *Superbad* and featuring half of its cast—it was clear that the bar was set. With all of the talent involved, maybe *Superbad* could clear it.

Thanks to Apatow's insistence, the film was suddenly being promoted within an inch of its life. In the most competitive summer they could've possibly have imagined—going head-to-head with Spider-Man, Harry Potter, Captain Jack Sparrow, Shrek, Optimus Prime, and Homer Simpson—only time would tell if *Superbad* could follow in the footsteps of its predecessors. But its odds looked pretty damn good. Plus, as a result of the test screenings, the filmmakers at the very least already knew *Superbad* worked as a whole. They knew which lines were getting the best reactions, and also which lines were consistently getting drowned out due to the laughter. Even Apatow—who was at the center of *Knocked Up*'s success—could sense something different was going on with *Superbad*, the likes of which he had never seen before.

"It makes *Knocked Up* seem so much less impressive when it is followed up by something like this," Apatow said shortly before the film came out. "I wish I was alone in an alley with this. I was trying to think of movies that get laughs this big. You really have to look at some of the great movies like *Airplane!* and *Young Frankenstein*. The only words I could use to describe it, because I've seen the movie with an audience a ton, is every single time, the place goes shithouse."[3]

Superbad was brutally honest by design. It felt as if the film was coming along at just the right time, as *The 40 Year-Old Virgin* and *Knocked Up* were proving that there is in fact an appetite for raunch comedies that aren't afraid to wear their heart on their sleeves. Maybe now would finally be the time for the raunchy high school comedy to return to its roots and make a long-awaited comeback.

Take a look at the John Hughes cinematic catalog, for instance. It's not just about the laughs—or the raunch—it's about the characters. One thing that sets his films apart from a *Porky's* is that their scripts leave plenty of room for character development. They don't feel like your average comedy that solely focuses on getting laughs—they actually have something to say. (Yes, there are also some brilliant jokes, too.)

It's the Hughes movies, in fact, that helped set the stage for the work that Apatow and his team ended up doing. Hughes was so inspirational to everyone of that generation that Rogen and Goldberg wrote a script for a film based on a treatment Hughes wrote decades earlier. With Apatow producing, *Drillbit Taylor* opened the following spring, and Hughes even got a final, albeit pseudonymous, onscreen credit as Edmond Dantes, in reference to the character from *The Count of Monte Cristo*. Even though they weren't directly working with their hero, they were technically associated all the same.

"John Hughes wrote some of the great outsider characters of all time," Apatow once said. "It's pretty ridiculous to hear people talk about the movies we've been doing, with outrageous humor and sweetness all combined, as if they were an original idea. I mean, it was all there first in John Hughes's films. Whether it's *Freaks and Geeks* or *Superbad*, the whole idea of having outsiders as the lead characters, that all started with Hughes."[4]

The film was also ripe for a generation that desperately needed to find representation on the screen. When Apatow did *Freaks and Geeks*, it was a period piece, meaning that it was steeped in nostalgia despite its realism. *Superbad*, on the other hand, was reflective of what it was like to be in high school in 2007. Despite the throwback undertones, the film was a modern high school comedy through and through. As a result, millennials took notice.

The millennial generation encompasses anyone who was born between 1981 and 1996. While Apatow and Mottola were part of Generation X, Rogen and Goldberg were born in 1982, thus making them millennials. Plus, Apatow's hallmark has always been harvesting new, younger talent—a badge he wears proudly. His films at the time held a special place in the hearts of that generation, the last one who would spend their adolescent years in a world before social media. These kids would still stay home on a Saturday night with their friends to watch Will Ferrell on *SNL*. Because what else would they do? They'd order a pizza, perhaps sneak some alcohol from their parents', liquor cabinet, and have some laughs. As a result, when Ferrell made the transition to making films, the millennials followed. When Apatow branched off and started making films of his own, they followed him, too.

For the first time, teenagers and twentysomethings could see their brand of humor represented on the big screen. It's crazy to think that in a world where a show like *South Park* was holding court on Comedy Central, it took as long as it did for films to catch up. While *Anchorman* and *Talladega Nights* both felt like they were still within the "safe zone" of PG-13 comedies, there was still an air of freshness to them. We were seeing characters who were more flawed—in an un-self-aware way—than what we had seen before. Then with films like *Old School*, *The 40 Year-Old Virgin*, and *Knocked Up*, it felt like they were taking their brand of humor to the next level. It was just what that generation was looking for. The one thing that hadn't yet been explored within the Apatow camp was the thing that all of those teenagers knew best: high school. With *Superbad*, that would all change.

The premiere was held at the iconic Grauman's Chinese Theater in Hollywood, California. It was a star-studded event, and there was excitement in the air, emitting not just from the crowd but especially from those who made *Superbad*. While comedies can sometimes hit or miss at premieres, no one seemed to be worrying about it. To put it frankly, it was the place to be on August 13, 2007. The vibe inside the room was so joyous and excited that Amy Pascal had to ask the crowd to quiet down twice so she could bring up Apatow to introduce the film.

"Thank you for coming and for getting dressed up to hear more [penis] jokes than you've ever heard in your life," Apatow told the crowd that night. "The last time I was up here it was for the premiere of *The Cable Guy*. I loved that movie, and I hope that nobody gets fired after this."[5]

After the adrenaline-filled screening, the afterparty was held at the Roosevelt Hotel across the street, with the *LA Times* saying the vibe felt like attending "a rich kid's graduation party." Not only was there an open bar, but in the spirit of the film, there were also some kegs. Sadly, no laundry detergent bottles filled with alcohol were to be found. But there was a photo booth where you could print your own fake ID. As those who were at the premiere found it, the overall vibe was celebratory. The party turned into an all-night affair, during which Rogen and Mintz-Plasse managed to smoke a joint with singer-songwriter Ben Harper at one point. It went on until four in the morning, when they essentially got kicked out of their own party.[6]

They had every reason to celebrate, though. While they didn't yet know how *Superbad* would fare at the box office, everything was still pointing in the direction of it being a smash hit. Unless some last-minute upset took everyone by surprise, *Superbad* could become the biggest comedy of the year. Pretty soon, that hope would be realized: the film opened number one at the box office, taking in $33 million its opening weekend, well surpassing its $20 million budget. Hardly anyone in the industry was surprised by this news. Furthermore, the consensus among critics was that the film was a hit. It's hard to get critics to agree nearly universally on anything, let alone a comedy. Yet critics were responding to the film just like audiences were.

"Superbad is a four-letter raunch-a-rama with a heart, and an inordinate interest in other key organs," Roger Ebert wrote, perhaps the most famous film critic of his time, or any other time for that matter. He continued, "It has that unchained air of getting away with something. In its very raunchiness, it finds truth, because if you know nothing about sex, how can you be tasteful and sophisticated on the subject?"[7] *New York Magazine* wrote that "*Superbad* might be the most provocative teen sex comedy ever made," adding that "it is certainly one of the most convulsively funny."[8] And *Newsweek* wrote, "Almost everyone in Hollywood is predicting that 'Superbad,' a new high-school comedy from the makers of '*Knocked Up*,' will be the sleeper hit of the summer, which raises the question: can a movie really be a sleeper hit if no one is asleep about it?"[9]

That last review raises a good point. To call it a "sleeper hit" would mean you hadn't been paying attention. There was heavy awareness right as the film was coming out, meaning that it couldn't possibly be defined as a sleeper hit. Everybody had been tracking *Superbad* ever since they saw how *Anchorman*, *Talladega Nights*, *The 40 Year-Old Virgin*, and *Knocked Up* performed, and since Apatow had Sony dump more money into the marketing budget. Also *Superbad* was made with a lot of the same folks as these films. It had all of the ingredients, all of the positive press, and all of the signs firmly pointing to its success. Nobody was sleeping on *Superbad*. The test scores were through the roof, and the studio was firmly behind it a thousand percent. There was no escaping it: the movie was simply going to be a bona fide smash. And that's precisely what happened.

Superbad was at the forefront of the summer comedy blockbuster movement. The film wound up grossing over $170 million at the box office. For any film with a $20 million budget, that's quite an accomplishment. But when you consider the fact that the film starred a cast of practical unknowns—or "hardly knowns"—success on that magnitude is about as rare as it comes in Hollywood.

"It was a moment when R-rated comedies sort of came roaring back," Tolmach says of the film's success. "I think it was great for the business. There was this new generation of comedians writing and producing and directing movies. And that's the thing about *Superbad*. It's not just a goofy high school movie. It's so authentic and it has integrity."[10]

It was a time when everyone was going to the movies to see the latest superhero epic. So the fact that the film—as well as *Knocked Up* before it—managed to generate as much money as it did at the box office speaks to the hunger for comedies of this caliber. With such staunch competition, these films starring nobodies held their own against movies that more than quadrupled their budget. More than anything else, such success had a lot to do with what they were offering. You wouldn't go see *Harry Potter and the Order of the Phoenix* if you were in search of a good laugh, but if that's what you needed, you knew *Superbad* was where to get one.

After the film was released, MacIsaac got a phone call from Amy Pascal congratulating her on the film's success. The importance of having the president of Sony call her didn't really dawn on her at first. When she told her agent, the news was met with disbelief. It was at this moment that it all finally started to click into place for MacIsaac, and she realized that the film must have been doing well.

One person who didn't see *Superbad* as being a sleeper hit was Seth Rogen, who, for years, was told that it would never work. But

Rogen got the last laugh. He was riding high at this moment, with two films raking in enormous amounts of money within two months of each other, one of which featured him as the lead. While both Rogen's and *Superbad*'s success hardly happened overnight—he spent nearly ten years working on *Superbad*—he always knew that if it did ever get made, it would work. It couldn't *not* work, as far as he saw it.

"I don't want to say we expected it," says Rogen, "but it's like, *Yes. That's what you get when you make the movie that we've said should've been made this whole time.* It had this—not like 'We told you so'— but, like, *Yes. We knew this is what would happen.*"[11]

Goldberg adds, "Before we ever pitched the movie to anybody, we were like, *You'll do stand-up. I'll be a lifeguard. We'll make $10,000, buy a camera, and make it in Vancouver.* And even with that version, we were like, *It's not going to be like a giant movie in theaters, but it'll be a good movie.* We just always believed that it'd be a good movie."[12]

Superbad was doing the impossible. With the exception of *Borat*, there hadn't been a whole lot of comedies that were driving teenagers and twentysomethings off the couch and back into movie theaters. Even before the advent of streaming, the younger generation was spending more and more time at home on the internet. It wasn't as easy to get someone to come out of self-inflicted hibernation and be around other people. YouTube was still in its earliest iteration, and people were spending an increasing amount of time watching whatever they could find there. If you were going to get people to keep going to theaters, you had to present them with a really good reason to do so. Apatow made the film inescapable, building up the hype to where you couldn't miss what many were calling "the raunchiest film in years," or "the funniest film since *Animal House*." You just had to see it for yourself. *Superbad* was basically acting as its own publicist.

Baumann recalls, "I remember when it really dawned on me was when the film was coming out and seeing the publicity team and billboards and lines around the block to see the film. It was surreal. That's when I actually realized the full size of the film and what it was going to become."[13]

The internet was increasingly helpful as a marketing tool. Just like how MySpace was utilized to find McLovin, Sony embraced the internet as part of its grassroots campaign. It proved a useful tool for 20th Century Fox earlier that summer with *The Simpsons Movie*—with the Spider-Pig scene being viewed millions of times that summer alone. Sony turned to that same strategy by uploading *Superbad* clips onto YouTube and creating MySpace profiles for the characters. The studio was also able to introduce an online red-band trailer, which is basically an uncensored trailer. "The R-rated trailer has been sort of the biggest marketing thing they could have done," Hill said at the time. "The Internet has been the biggest way to get the word out about the movie and what the movie is actually like."[14]

"I think the Sony marketing people are very savvy," says Mottola. "They were earlier than a lot of other companies to realize that the youth market had changed radically and how to communicate to them had changed radically. They realized that young people weren't opening up the *New York Times* to look at ads. They were really smart about how they did it. Instead of just blasting money out of a hose, they really did it strategically."[15]

You couldn't go anywhere without hearing teenagers and early twentysomethings screaming "I am McLovin!" at the top of their lungs. Seemingly overnight, McLovin's goofy fake ID completely overtook Borat as the face of that moment in comedy. It got to the point where it was just unavoidable. Everywhere you went in the summer of 2007, it was almost guaranteed that you'd bump into someone wearing a McLovin T-shirt. By Christmas, the McLovin fake IDs became a staple of every Hot Topic or Spencer's, or wherever else you could find novelty items. Only the coolest kids had a McLovin decal on their cars.

But it wasn't just McLovin that was resonating with the youth. It was the film's message as a whole. It encouraged high schoolers that it was okay to be open with your feelings in a world where culture would be quick to dismiss something "men" didn't do. It showed audiences how ridiculous it was that you couldn't tell your best friend that you loved them.

Apatow recalls, "I remember when it came out, James L. Brooks saw the movie and sent me a really kind note that said that he went to it with his son—who was in high school—and a bunch of his friends. And it felt like it was the first time that they all realized that they loved each other. And to me, as someone who has been so inspired by him, that was the best compliment the film could have received."[16]

"The great romance of your youth is your best friend at that age," Hill said years later in an interview. "But when a comedy takes you from laughing your ass off to feeling something without a moment's notice—that's just different. It just is."[17]

It wasn't just the younger generation that were latching on to *Superbad*, either. About 40 percent of *Superbad*'s earliest grosses were courtesy of people over thirty. The conceit of a high school movie that both millennials and older generations can relate to was turning out to be a profitable idea.

McLovin wound up infiltrating pop culture, finding a sizeable presence in rap songs and pretty much any type of apparel you could think of. While comedy often has an expiration date, *Superbad* clearly did not. Even while shooting the film, the cast and crew had a strong sense that Mintz-Plasse would be closely identified with McLovin once the film came out.

Christopher Mintz-Plasse was newly eighteen by the time of the film's release. He and Cera—who was then nineteen—were in the precise age bracket as their audience; they were two stars in the biggest movie in the world, unable to go into a bar and drink themselves, just like their onscreen counterparts. The attention they started getting on the street mirrored the film's success. Seemingly overnight, they became the coolest guys around, and everybody wanted to get—uncomfortably—close to them.

"I remember the weekend after going to Chipotle," recalls Mintz-Plasse. "I got recognized and a girl would like run over and climb over my friends to try and touch me and try to grab me. And I would run out of the Chipotle, and all of their friends would run after me. I'd get in the car and one of the guys put his finger through his pants and was like 'I got a boner! I got a boner!'" That specific refrain, of course, is in direct reference to one of Fogell's most memorable lines during his sex scene with Aviva Baumann as Nicola. To someone who isn't used to that sort of attention—to go overnight from being a complete unknown to people chasing you down the street—it can be a lot to deal with. Couple that with being as young as Mintz-Plasse was at the time and you can understand his considerable discomfort.[18]

He wasn't alone when it came to getting attention, though. His *Superbad* cohorts were just as easily spotted out in public. Cera has his own story about encountering a guy in a bar in Toronto who wanted to beat him up before *Superbad* came out. Next time he saw Cera, he sidled up next to him and tried to befriend him, going as far as offering to join Cera next time he has to fly to Los Angeles.[19]

"The day *Superbad* came out was literally the day I became recognizable," Hill later said. "I literally couldn't walk around the neighborhood anymore without being stopped all the time, which was flattering but odd. One minute, you're just that guy walking around; and the next, you're suddenly interesting. It's strange to have mothers with baby carriages or little old ladies saying, 'Are you the guy in that movie with the big party at the end of it?' Really? Those women saw the movie? The little kids standing next to them saw the film, too?"[20]

It wasn't limited to the three leads, either. Everyone in the film was now part of the public consciousness. By the time *Superbad* came out, Hader was about to enter his third season on *Saturday Night Live*. Living in New York, he would occasionally get someone shouting "Hey *SNL!*" at him on the street. But as soon as the film came out, he sensed an immediate shift. Within twenty-four hours of the film's release, he had cops asking him "Where's McLovin??" That's how quickly everything happened.[21]

While the cast was getting a great deal of attention for their work, *Superbad* also culminated quite a big year for Seth Rogen and Judd Apatow; by the end of the summer, they were bona fide comedy superstars. Having one hit movie is reason enough to celebrate. But when you've got two in a single year—with more on the way—you find yourself breathing only the finest rarified air. As a result, *GQ* listed Apatow, Cera, Rogen, and Hill as part of their annual Men of the Year, calling them the "comedy mafia." So much attention was being paid to them that you couldn't ignore it if you tried: they were onboard an unstoppable train.

"When *The 40 Year-Old Virgin* came out, I was in North Carolina producing *Talladega Nights*," Apatow recalls. "I was so busy working on the film that I didn't really experience its success that much. Just because we were deep in a very complicated project. So the summer of *Knocked Up* and *Superbad* was really fun because I was around for the premieres and all of the press. There was a lot more in the media about those projects. We did all the talk shows. So it was a really fun victory lap."[22]

Rogen and Apatow were around to do all the press for their two films stateside. Then once *Superbad* hit theaters, they kept their eye on it from afar. As Rogen later remembered, "I remember I was gone. Me and Judd were promoting *Knocked Up* overseas when the movie came out in theaters. And I look back and I had no concept that the movie was doing well or it was being well received. I didn't care at all at the time."[23]

Advertising a movie with three unknown stars wasn't initially going to be easy. If anyone in the film was anywhere close to a household name—such as Seth Rogen and Bill Hader—it was only within the year leading up to the film's release. When you need to market a film with three unknown actors, the only way you can do that is to put them everywhere. To help raise awareness, Jonah Hill, Michael Cera, and Christopher Mintz-Plasse were sent on a media blitz where they were doing anything and everything to make the film's presence—and their own—known. Cera compared this period of his life to being strapped to a "publicity rocket."[24]

Studios have to bring their product to the consumers to raise awareness for it, and Hollywood did so via the "movie roadshow" for many years. For the first half of the twentieth century, movie stars couldn't go on *The Tonight Show* or do some print or podcast interviews to fulfill their contractual requirements in promoting their latest projects; instead, stars of yesteryear had to rely on making public appearances across the country. This is why you'd see—for instance—Jerry Lewis traveling far and wide to various movie theaters to publicize something like *The Nutty Professor*. Sony brought this model back for *Superbad*.

The three leads were sent to college campuses all across the country to do free screenings and Q and As. It was an effective way to help raise their profiles among the audience that would be telling all their friends how funny *Superbad* is. Imagine actually being able to see a movie and then hang out with the actors afterward. Then, turning to social media, those college kids could go onto MySpace or Facebook and talk about how funny the movie was, further encouraging their friends to see it. From a marketing standpoint it was actually pretty genius, long before hashtags were a thing. As Tolmach would later say, "This is not your standard having a junket at the Four Seasons plan. It was really hitting the ground and finding people."[25]

"I went on a little press tour with Jonah, Michael, and Chris," Hader reflected years later. "I went to Atlanta and Florida with them, and that was a lot of fun. I always said I feel like I'm Josh Brolin in *The Goonies*. Like I was just like a little older with all these teenagers and they were running around and acting crazy. And just doing bits that no one found funny except for us."[26]

As for interviews, they went on every program that would have them, including *The Today Show*, *The Late Show with David Letterman*, *TRL*, *The Late Late Show with Craig Ferguson*, *Late Night with Conan O'Brien*, and the Teen Choice Awards, and would sit down with every journalist who would look in their direction. They played miniature golf on *Good Morning America* (Mintz-Plasse won) and encountered snakes (which Hill is incredibly afraid of) on *The Tonight Show with Jay Leno*.

Then the press tour moved overseas to basically every country that they could promote in, in a massive push that lasted weeks. Hill, Cera, and Mintz-Plasse shook every hand as if they were running for office. The trio found themselves in London, Scotland, Australia, Germany, Spain, and all over the rest of Europe. For every country they brought the movie to, the audience related to the film differently. During the tender moment at the end of the film between Seth and Evan in sleeping bags, Italians just laughed, thinking that was the joke. Some other countries loved it. Then there were those that didn't know what to make of it. Mintz-Plasse always went out of his way on the press tour to pop his head into the theater as they were screening one particular moment of the film: the "I've got a boner" scene. It didn't matter if it was in Germany or Australia or Spain, that line killed in every language.[27, 28]

"I got to see the film in another language," says Aviva Baumann, who was shooting another film in Berlin when *Superbad* came out. "That blew my mind, too. To see how the comedy translated to a foreign audience, and every joke landed just the same."[29]

Each country also has its own take on translating film titles. Oftentimes, the title of an American movie will be changed for other countries to something that makes more sense to the audience. The translations of *Superbad* range from amusing to just bizarre. The film is known as *Supercool* in Argentina, *Supergrave* in Belgium, *Superbad: Pigs behind Desks* in Italy, *Superbad: Or Why Is Sex Funny?* in Hungary, and *Superhorny* in Spain.[30]

Also in Spain, there was a real push behind the actress who dubbed Emma Stone's part, Michelle Jenner. Jenner was on a Spanish series at the time titled *Los hombres de Paco*, and the producers of that show really wanted her to be part of the film's marketing in Spain. They went so far as to remove Emma Stone from the poster and added Jenner in Stone's place, with the three guys looking confused under her legs. She even did red carpet appearances alongside the guys, whom she had never met. This practice is unheard of, where someone who dubbed another actress in a film would be touted as the star when you don't even see their face on camera. But that's just one of the concessions you sometimes have to make in order to promote an American film—particularly an American comedy that is so dialogue heavy—overseas. They were willing to try anything to get young people into seats.

Doing so much press is draining work, as if there's anything else you can possibly say about your project that you haven't already. The stars were asked the same questions time and time again, and they gave the same answers about how they got involved in the film, how much they resemble their characters, whether or not they really had a fake ID, what their high school experience was like, and so forth. At a certain point, they were at their best in interviews where they hardly mentioned the film at all, and would instead talk at length about Subway sandwiches or sex expert Sue Johanson. They grasped at these kinds of straws to keep themselves entertained, as they were clearly getting exhausted. Hill actually told a radio DJ early on, "This tour has made me realize how people in rock bands are cool and I'm lame. I'm *tired*." This interview occurred before the film even came out, and before they were sent on their monthslong world tour. So one can only imagine how much more intense it got before they were finally done.[31]

It was that type of tired energy that made its way into a comedy bit that Hill and Cera did with Edgar Wright, who wasn't that well-known yet in the United States beyond being the director of *Shaun of the Dead*. The duo sat down with Wright, who was posing as a journalist, for a bit that circulated online. Wright asks the actors what question they're most sick of, to which they respond, "Probably like 'What does it mean to be Superbad?'" He then asks, "But what *does* it mean to be Superbad?" He goes on to ask them how it feels now that they've peaked, whether Hill feels it is "important to be unattractive to be funny," and can "skinny people be funny?" His final jab—"What will you do when your career is over in a couple of months?"—results in Hill storming off.[32]

The clip was intended as a viral video, a concept that studios had yet to fully embrace. The idea of going "viral" was still new to many, and this was among the earliest attempts. By and large, the experiment worked. The average American didn't know who Edgar Wright was, so he was the perfect foil. As Apatow recalls, this new grassroots approach was helpful in launching the film.[33]

The comedy bit perfectly sums up the very real experience of what it was like on the press tour. You can practically feel Hill unleashing everything he wishes he could express during the endless months of press. Having to answer the same questions time and time again was clearly getting to the three leads, which you can start to see coming through in later interviews. It's important to note that they always remained polite and cordial, no matter how much press they had to do. But unraveling, just as Hill did in the fake clip, was a distinct possibility. "I think at some point," says Apatow, "everyone realized that they had pushed them too hard. They really ran out of gas at some point and were flying all over the country spreading the word."[34]

Tolmach adds, "Those [junkets] are exhausting. There was just so much excitement around [the film]. They may have felt [exhausted], but for us, I remember feeling, 'Wow. They have tapped into this whole audience of this younger generation, who is just rabid for this and who gets them. And who they get.' It was the beginning of that relationship that all those guys had with their audience."[35]

The press tour did manage to bring the trio closer together. They were able to share an experience with one another that most people wouldn't be able to relate to. Just as a film shoot can be a bonding experience, a rigorous press tour can generate the same results. They were being flown all around the world on the studio's dime, spending hours on a couch talking to a never-ending stream of journalists, and ending their days standing at the back of a darkened movie theater while waiting to get introduced for a Q and A. They could've either ended up despising one another or growing closer together. Luckily, for Hill, Cera, and Mintz-Plasse, it was the latter.

"If I think back to myself in my teenage years," recalls Cera years later, "it's alarming. I have this footage of us from the *Superbad* press tour, and even watching that and looking at myself when I was like nineteen, it's really disturbing." He added, "I had this very sudden exposure to people knowing who I was, which made everything even more confusing just on a day-to-day, existing basis."[36]

You couldn't replicate the momentum or the heights that *Superbad* reached upon its release if you tried. It's once-in-a-lifetime, lightning-in-a-bottle type stuff. In a summer that was loaded with cinematic options, the film proved that it could hold its own in the big leagues. It became the cool, hip thing to see. Everybody was talking about it. It just so happens that in the years that followed, the *Superbad* love grew even stronger.

12

The Six Degrees of *Superbad*

In the mid-2000s, film studios were putting a lot of stock in DVD extras. There was a notion that if you packed more "bang for your buck" into a release, you could charge even more and people would be willing to pay. This was proven correct, as the DVD market would basically allow studios to have a second bite at the apple as people who already saw the film in theaters purchased the films for home entertainment. Most DVD releases had a standard "making-of" featurette, a blooper reel, deleted scenes, and perhaps a director's commentary.

Apatow and his crew, meanwhile, were embracing the format like few others. Not only did they have a main behind-the-scenes featurette, but they also spent a lot of extra time filming extras just for home media. In addition to Line-O-Rama, which showcased a revolving door of improvisations on a single line of dialogue, you could see Seth Rogen getting drunk with Stormy Daniels on *The 40 Year-Old Virgin*, or Jay Baruchel go on roller coasters in a featurette on the *Knocked Up* DVD. This strategy was to make sure the home audience got their money's worth in terms of content. So many special features consist of either running around with a camera and capturing things as they happen or going to extreme lengths with high-concept inside jokes for the DVDs. One of these instances is a satirical documentary for *Knocked Up*, where Apatow had many of his famous friends—including Michael Cera, Justin Long, David

Krumholtz, Bill Hader, and Orlando Bloom—sit in on a scene as Rogen's character, before Apatow would then take the actor aside and fire them on camera. All this was simply meta content designed specifically for the biggest comedy nerds.

During this era, the "hip" thing to do was release an "unrated" version of your film when it came out on DVD. One way to capitalize on this was to have two separate releases: the theatrical release, which would feature exactly what you saw in theaters, and the "unrated" or "extended" version, which would essentially be a director's cut. What usually happened is that a bunch of deleted scenes would simply be added back into the film. Most times, what was featured in the "unrated" cut wasn't even too wild for theaters, although occasionally it was footage that the MPA forced the filmmakers to remove. It was all just a marketing ploy, truthfully. It usually worked pretty well.

In the case of *Superbad*, there is only about seven additional minutes of material added to the extended cut. This includes a flashback fantasy sequence with Jules, Evan in woodshop class, and various other non sequiturs that are fun but don't really add anything to the story. *The 40 Year-Old Virgin* had closer to seventeen minutes of new material. As a lot of people would buy the extended cut and not the theatrical cut, there are people out there who believe the longer incarnation of the film is how it was initially intended to be. As for Mottola, he always prefers the original cut. "The film was better without those additional seven minutes," he says.[1]

Surprisingly, there is even an additional twelve minutes of material that didn't make it into the extended version. A lot of this was expendable footage, featuring nothing that really moved the plot along one way or the other. There's more of Seth bringing alcohol to the party, Fogell and the cops, and an entire new backstory for Officer Slater's wife. One exception to this, however, is a sequence that gives us further insight into who Seth really is. In it Seth and Evan attempt to steal alcohol from Evan's parents before realizing that the alcohol had already been replaced with water. At the end of the scene, Seth throws down the bottle in frustration. Evan forces him throw it away and not litter in front of his house, and then point-blank calls him out, asking him, "Why are you doing this all the time?" Seth lowers his guard and apologizes, saying, "I'm just having a shitty day, man. It's not about you. It's just sometimes I don't know how to take out my anger." This shows us that Seth's "macho anger" is really just a facade.[2]

For *Superbad*, the special features include the auditions for Hill, Cera, and Mintz-Plasse, as well as an extended look at the making of the opening dancing montage, the table reads from 2002 with Rogen and Jason Segel, those with the final cast in 2006, a prank on Hill involving snakes, a documentary about the real McLovin, Wright's press junket encounter, an extended version of the Vag-Tastic Voyage from the film, a mock show called *Cop Car Confessions* starring Rogen and Hader alongside famous friends, and a look at the making of the music of *Superbad*. If you liked special features beyond your wildest dreams, this was the version for you.

Plus, there is a mock featurette called *Everyone Hates Michael Cera* that shows Cera pissing everyone off on set. According to Cera, "There was a guy named Greg Cohen who was tasked with doing everything sort of like behind the scenes in Judd Apatow world around that time. Greg's job was to come up with things to make for behind the scenes." The *Everyone Hates Michael Cera* idea was most likely Evan Goldberg's idea, says Cera.[3]

Another staple of every 1990s and 2000s DVD that was worth getting was the commentary. A lot of commentaries feature insight into how a certain project got made, perfect for any cinephile or inspiring filmmaker. You might hear the director talking about camera angles or certain obstacles with a particular scene and how they overcame them. When they did the commentary for *The 40 Year-Old Virgin*, however, the entire cast and crew gathered in the room together, trying to one-up one another for laughs—you could argue that it was just as funny as the movie itself. *Superbad* was no different. When you get Greg Mottola, Judd Apatow, Jonah Hill, Michael Cera, Seth Rogen, Evan Goldberg, and Christopher Mintz-Plasse into one place to record a commentary, you know it's going to be a fun time.

Due to scheduling complications, though, the commentary featured the actors split up in two locations: Rogen, Goldberg, Mintz-Plasse, and Cera were in Los Angeles while Apatow, Hill, and Mottola were in New York. Apatow had brought with him his nine-year-old daughter Maude, and had to leave halfway through to do press for the film. Apatow used this opportunity to create even more meta comedy within the film's commentary. "Also here is my daughter Maude, who is nine," Apatow announces. "She's not wearing headphones, so she can't hear, but when we get to the male genital scene, I'm going to cover her eyes. But still she can hear what Jonah and Greg are saying, so no cursing on the New York side please."

During the session, which felt a lot like you were a fly on the wall during an intimate hang among friends, Hill accidentally slipped and cursed multiple times. Apatow apparently covered his daughter's eyes during the sexual antics of the home economics scene. But Apatow's big blowout came when Hill let one too many "fucks" slip, and he stormed off. Of course, none of it actually was real. Because Apatow had a hard stop in the middle of the commentary to return to his work doing press for the film, they decided to make his abrupt exit more interesting by staging a fake fight in the midst. The fight was so convincing that people still question its veracity. But it truly was all just for show, blurring the lines of what is real and what isn't.[4]

Ever the brilliant producer when it came to finding loopholes, Apatow would approach the studio during production and ask them to give him additional money to produce special features for the DVD. The studio would oblige, knowing he'd deliver a lot of great bonus content. Apatow would then take that money and put it into the film's actual budget and find other creative ways to get bonus features for less money. This is one of the many valuable lessons that Shauna Robertson learned from Apatow during their time working together.

"Basically, we never had enough money to make the movie," Apatow says. "And we would say to the studio if they gave us whatever number it was, that would give us two more days of shooting. And within those two days, we'll also be able to shoot a lot of additional material for the DVD extras. I think it was a bit of a con, but it also helped both the DVD extras and the movie. So I don't feel *that* guilty about it. Universal and Sony were very supportive of the concept of the marketing department paying a big hunk of money for DVD extras because we were all realizing that all of these weird, funny things we did would go online and get millions of hits, and that was a very valuable market."

Over time, the practice of overloading special features onto a DVD sort of went away. Mainly, studios realized that fewer people were buying the home media and instead renting or eventually streaming films. There was no longer a reason to monetize special features. So studios no longer shelled out that extra $800,000 to $1 million for bonus material.

Superbad had two home media releases: There was a standard DVD with some bonus features and a jam-packed DVD featuring all of the bonus features you could possibly imagine. The first week of its release alone—just in time for the holidays in early December 2007—generated $58 million, which is exceptional for a new release and returned nearly triple the film's overall budget. Between DVD and the brand-new Blu-ray format, the film wound up bringing in $140,977,695 for home media alone. For a movie made on a $20 million budget that had already made nearly $170 million in theaters, that was a win no matter how you look at it.

The legacy of *Superbad* continued to grow. Over the course of their careers, the cast and crew would cross paths on many occasions.

Most notably, a mini-*Superbad* reunion was built into 2013's *This Is the End*, written and directed by Rogen and Goldberg. The film saw Hill, Cera, and Mintz-Plasse playing exaggerated versions of themselves. Their first time onscreen together in six years features Cera blowing a handful of cocaine into Mintz-Plasse's face in a brief reunion scene.

In the mid- to late 2000s Apatow continued his tradition of getting the band back together for project after project. The "summer camp" experience was built into the fabric of his productions, both as producer and director, turning his work into a Marvel-type Cinematic Universe of comedy. Even though the characters didn't necessarily share the same universe, all of the actors definitely did, and the films were all better for it. For instance, immediately after making *Superbad*, Rogen starred in the film he cowrote with Goldberg and which Apatow produced, *Pineapple Express*. This weed-centered action film—which nobody initially wanted to make—costarred James Franco and Danny McBride, the latter of whom made a cameo in *Superbad*. Then there's Bill Hader and Joe Lo Truglio making their own cameos in the film. Like *Superbad*, *Pineapple Express* was a critical and box office smash hit, once again proving that Rogen and Goldberg were right about which ideas could work.

Call this career web the Six Degrees of *Superbad* if you must, filled with crossovers throughout various project. Rogen and Hill would team up again with Apatow for *Funny People*, with Hill also starring in the Apatow-produced *Get Him to the Greek* and *Forgetting Sarah Marshall*. Bill Hader was also in *Forgetting Sarah Marshall* and would go on to star in the Apatow-directed *Trainwreck*, as well as the Mottola-directed projects *Adventureland* and *Paul*, the latter of which costarred Seth Rogen. Rogen cast Mintz-Plasse in *Neighbors* before bringing Hill, Cera, and Bill Hader together for his 2016 animated film *Sausage Party*. Cera also reunited with Apatow and Mintz-Plasse for 2009's *Year One*. Emma Stone and Martha

MacIsaac costarred in *Battle of the Sexes*, but before that, MacIsaac also appeared in the film *For a Good Time Call*, which featured a cameo from Seth Rogen and was cowritten by his wife, Lauren Miller. Finally, in 2018, Emma Stone and Jonah Hill brought their chemistry to the small screen for Netflix's *Maniac*.

That map can get tangled when you're trying to keep track of how much the cast and crew of *Superbad* stayed within one another's orbits. That wasn't solely because the film was a box office smash, although that probably didn't hurt, either. More than anything, it was primarily because they all just enjoyed working together. Once you can find a rhythm with people you like, you'll want to surround yourself with that same energy again and again.

At the very center of this web is Rogen and Goldberg. Ever since they met as twelve-year-olds, the two men have been inseparable. They wrote their first screenplay together and are now powerhouses and business partners in the world of Hollywood together. As directors, they've collaborated on *This Is the End* and *The Interview*. As writers, they've penned *Pineapple Express*, *The Green Hornet*, *Sausage Party*, and *Teenage Mutant Ninja Turtles: Mutant Mayhem*. As producers, they've worked on countless projects, including *The Disaster Artist*, *An American Pickle*, *Blockers*, *Long Shot*, *Preacher*, *The Boys*, *Good Boys*, *Pam & Tommy*, and *Invincible*.

The title of the latter pretty accurately sums up their output as collaborators in the years that have followed *Superbad*. They've gone from being two young screenwriters who couldn't get a studio to take their film seriously to two guys who have more or less taken over Hollywood many times over. Given the subject matter of *The Interview*—which follows a talk show host who is enlisted by the government to kill Kim Jong Un—they were even at the center of an international incident that led to threats of revenge from North Korea. That's about as powerful as it gets. The fact that the two men still work so closely with each other gives the audience hope that the same could be said for the characters of Seth and Evan. Even though getting into different schools has the characters drifting apart physically, that's not to say that their friendship will be impacted as a result. Rogen and Goldberg are proof of how well two guys can work together for so many years.

"It's very weird and it's not lost on me that we have a very healthy, good working relationship with one another," Rogen said of their partnership. "I've seen a lot of writing partnerships—obviously as a writer, you know other people who are in partnerships. And I've seen a lot of others evaporate. Even people who have been together for years and years and years and years."[5]

The year that *Superbad* came out was a big year for the film's stars as well. Michael Cera especially had a hell of a 2007. In addition to his work in *Superbad*, he also starred in *Juno* alongside Elliot Page, which explored teenage pregnancy. Cera's overall likeable—yet awkward—charm made him poised to break out with *Superbad*'s younger audience. He got further geek cred in 2010 when he starred in Edgar Wright's *Scott Pilgrim vs. the World*. While the film didn't get nearly the same reaction as *Superbad* upon its release, it has secured its place in the pop culture canon and is now highly regarded as a cult classic.

At this point, Cera started making interesting choices, like starring in such independent films as *Crystal Fairy & the Magical Cactus* and *Magic Magic*, as well as doing Kenneth Lonergan plays on Broadway. He also went on to play Ken's best friend Allan in the box office juggernaut *Barbie*, which was the most talked-about film of 2023. But by and large he has been able to escape being typecast for one specific thing. Michael Cera was out to prove that he could be more than the shy and awkward guy that you'd see him play in some of his earliest roles.

Hill has also made some intriguing career choices. Riding high off of *Superbad*, he wouldn't have found it difficult to coast his way into becoming strictly one of the biggest comedy actors of the moment. In fact, he was even offered the role of Alan in *The Hangover* movies (which went to Zach Galifianakis). While nobody knew what a massive runaway hit that film would go on to be, it was a nice guaranteed payday for Hill to do something that seemed like the natural progression of starring in *Superbad*. Instead, he turned it down to do the John C. Reilly indie dramedy *Cyrus*. That sort of tells you everything you need to know about how Hill approached his post-*Superbad* career. While Rogen may be more generally looked to as a comedian, Hill fashioned himself into an actor who just so happened to make some comedies, like 2010's *Get Him to the Greek*, which saw him partnering with Russell Brand. But he wasn't afraid to tackle more challenging parts.

Aside from *Cyrus*, the first time most of us really took note of this transition for Hill was with 2011's *Moneyball*. The film paired him up with Brad Pitt, in which Hill played Peter Brand, which was a composite of multiple different assistants that Billy Beane had, most notably Paul DePodesta. The performance wound up getting him his first Academy Award nomination. After a successful comedy alongside Channing Tatum in *21 Jump Street*, he got his second Academy Award nomination for Martin Scorsese's *The Wolf of Wall Street*. Hill also eventually got behind the camera, directing the nostalgia skater dramedy *Mid90s* and the documentary *Stutz* about his psychiatrist.

Of course, Hill was not the only one whose career brought him to the Academy Awards. After *Superbad*, Emma Stone went on to costar in 2009's *Zombieland* before landing her own breakout comedy, *Easy A*. She quickly transitioned to more dramatic fare after that, including 2011's *The Help*. After entering the franchise world with *The Amazing Spider-Man* film series, she played the role of Mia Dolan in *La La Land*. The film was met with critical praise for Stone and landed her the Academy Award for Best Actress. Her career trajectory has been similar to Hill's and Cera's, and she's starred in a variety of different projects, ranging from blockbusters to indie darlings. Her turn in 2023's *Poor Things* won her acclaim from critics and audiences alike, as well as a second Oscar. Whether she's starring in *The Favourite* or Disney's *Cruella*, Emma Stone has proven that anything she does will be interesting.

Then there's Christopher Mintz-Plasse. If there's any actor in *Superbad* that ran the risk of being typecast, it'd be him. It's no secret that when an actor becomes so identified with a certain role, it's hard to break free from that. The more successful and widely known a particular character becomes, the harder it is to escape it. It's sort of like Frankenstein's monster in that respect, and Mintz-Plasse easily could've had a Frankenstein's monster with McLovin.

Thankfully, he was cast against type immediately following *Superbad*, stealing his scenes in David Wain's *Role Models* opposite Paul Rudd and Seann William Scott. In it he plays a loner, reserved and aloof, with remarkably less confidence than Fogell. Like *Superbad*, *Role Models* has also become a favorite for comedy fans. After pairing back up with Cera in *Year One*, Mintz-Plasse found himself in a few successful films that spawned franchises of their own, including *Kick-Ass*, *Trolls*, and *How to Train Your Dragon*, which also costarred Hill. He worked with Rogen again in *Neighbors* and *Neighbors 2* and was part of the Oscar-nominated *Promising Young Woman* and has also proven himself to be a talented musician in two bands: first as a drummer in the *Young Rapscallions* then as a bass guitarist in *Bear on Fire*.

When Hader joined the cast of *Superbad*, he was one of the most recognizable names attached. Despite the fact that it was still relatively early in his *Saturday Night Live* tenure—he was about to enter his third season as a cast member when the film came out—he had already built up a number of credits. In addition to his small role in *Knocked Up*, Hader could also be seen that same summer starring alongside Andy Samberg in *Hot Rod*. Following *Superbad* his star only continued to rise. In the years that followed, he appeared in *Tropic Thunder*, *Cloudy with a Chance of Meatballs*, *Inside Out*, *The Skeleton Twins*, *It Chapter Two*, and the hit HBO series *Barry*, for which he won an Emmy Award.

As for Martha MacIsaac, she has continued to steadily work in both the United States as well as Canada. Some of her post-*Superbad* film and TV credits include the 2009 remake of *The Last House on the Left*, *Battle of the Sexes*, *For a Good Time Call*, Val Kilmer's *The Thaw*, *Unicorn Store*, *Greek*, and *Family Guy*.

It's no coincidence that everyone from *Superbad* kept winding up in one another's orbits. Yes, it shows what a small world Hollywood truly is. But much of that can be attributed to the close-knit environment that was cultivated for the film on set. It's one that Hill went out of his way to try to create when he directed his own film, *Mid90s*. It also helps that everyone involved with *Superbad* genuinely likes working together.

"I think certain people are just very loose and funny and can improvise and are comfortable with who they are and let their humanity and vulnerability shine through," Apatow once said about his tendency to work with the same people. "And we tend to be drawn to people like that."[6]

Superbad was such a big hit that everyone immediately found themselves in the public eye, whether they wanted to be or not. As Michael Cera would later recall, he found it so challenging that he went out of his way to "stop taking jobs that would make me famous." That's how uncomfortable it made him. He later said, "I didn't know how to handle walking down the street. Fame makes you very uncomfortable in your own skin, and makes you paranoid and weird. There were lots of great things about it, and I met a lot of amazing people, but there's a lot of bad energies, too, ones that I was not equipped to handle."[7]

It wasn't just the cast that immediately reaped the benefits of fame, either. Before *Superbad*, Greg Mottola was working in television.

It had been ten years since he had made *The Daytrippers* in 1997. *Superbad* afforded him the opportunity to make his next film, *Adventureland*, which he had actually already written. But on the tails of *Superbad* coming out—with all of the buzz it generated—he was able to get it picked up by Miramax. This time, mercifully, he didn't have to deal with Harvey Weinstein trying to change the ending.

"My only regret there is they then tried to sell it as *Superbad*, which it clearly is not for anyone who has ever seen it," says Mottola of how *Adventureland* was marketed. "I think that kind of hurt the movie in a way because people felt lied to. *Superbad* audiences were like *This isn't 'Superbad.'* But it was never meant to be."[8]

When a film is this successful and the cast still manages to like one another as much as this one does at the end of it, the first question that comes to mind is "When is the sequel coming out?" While their paths have continually crossed over the years, by and large, most people involved with the film remain convinced that it should be a one-and-done sort of deal and there shouldn't be a sequel. Rogen is the first to shut down any talks of a sequel, having said, "It would not be better. It just wouldn't be. I would make a movie with all these same people. I would write another movie with Evan that Greg Mottola directs starring me and Jonah and Michael and Emma and Martha and Chris and Bill. But it shouldn't be *Superbad*."[9]

Cera agrees with that sentiment, having stated that he would be up for doing anything with that group of people, with the exception of redoing or following up *Superbad*. Some, however, think it might be fun, but only under the right circumstances. Hill wouldn't mind taking Seth and Evan from being high school seniors to being literal seniors in an assisted living home. "That's the only way I would ever make it."[10]

One person who didn't think they had to wait that long was Judd Apatow. He was pushing for a sequel right away about Seth flunking out of college and showing up to visit Evan. Mottola, however, said that if they had done a sequel—which he didn't want to do—he'd have the characters shift around a bit. So you'd have a film that features Evan and Officer Slater hanging out.[11]

Unless Rogen and Goldberg find a way to justify a second bite at the apple, it's all but guaranteed that we've seen the last of Seth and Evan. But as much as the cast and crew has continued to work together over the years, one could argue that there's been various elements of "spiritual sequels" underlying a lot of the subsequent projects, such as the scene featuring Hill, Cera, and Mintz-Plasse in *This Is the End*. For every sequel that works, there's nearly a thousand sequels that don't work. The audience's enthusiasm for a sequel isn't enough to carry an entire film if there isn't a story to back it up. So perhaps it's best to just leave *Superbad* alone and be grateful that all of the stars managed to align at one time.

13

A New Generation

As times change, so does the way in which we examine art from years past. We've seen scenarios time and time again where once-successful comedies don't necessarily hold up when viewed through a modern lens. Many raunchy 1980s comedies, like *Revenge of the Nerds*, are proof of this. While *Revenge* was successful enough at the time to generate multiple sequels, it's pretty safe to assume that the filmmakers wouldn't get away with (nor would they want to film) scenes where the nerds spy on girls as they're changing or where one character puts on a mask and then sleeps with a cheerleader while pretending to be someone else. It's made even worse when the masked character is supposed to be the good guy in the movie, someone you're supposed to root for.

High school comedies, more than just about every other subgenre, are subject to this kind of scrutiny. This is because the movies emulate the sort of matter-of-fact way high schoolers talk. Back in 2007, you couldn't walk down the halls of a school without overhearing someone decry that something was "so gay," proclaiming "no homo," or tagging every other statement with "your mom." That doesn't mean it was okay, but it was the reality of being in school during that time.

That isn't to say *Superbad* is completely devoid of dated language. The character of Seth has moments where he utilizes language that probably wouldn't have made it into the film if it were made today, even though it unfortunately was completely authentic for what a high schooler would've said during that era. For instance, there are multiple moments in the film where Seth refers to Fogell as a "faggot" or "retard." For some, his discussion with Evan on the soccer field also raises questions when viewed through a modern lens: the whole idea of getting your crush alcohol for the sole purpose of sleeping with her probably wouldn't make it into a commercial comedy today, let alone become a trailer moment.

Says Mottola, "I think if the movie came out now, there'd be a lot of pushback and think pieces and arguments about what that character is saying. I would argue that the character—and it's key to how Jonah played it—has been exposed to a lot of toxic male behavior in the world and popular culture and his peer group. And he mistakenly thinks that's the way to be and that women might actually want you to be that way. I think it's so clear in Jonah's performance that this kid is scared and that he does not know what he's talking about and that he's trying to navigate something that he doesn't understand. And his friend is much more sensitive and hesitant to go with him on these physical journeys or verbal journeys. And by the end of the movie, they've kind of had some realizations about that's not who they are."[1]

Part of what helps balance things out is that it's not the filmmakers' point of view—it's clearly the character. Seth is never supposed to be perfect. He is flawed, just as he was written to be. You're not supposed to idolize him or look up to him, as he makes the wrong choices and acts inappropriately in certain situations. His is a complicated, immature character who talks a big game but doesn't realize that women aren't into that aggressive approach. It's painfully obvious that he still has much growing up to do, which is not unlike most eighteen-year-olds who are about to enter the real world. In certain scenes, we see that his rough exterior is masking someone who's much more vulnerable than what is on the surface. His words serve as an emotional shield.

This fails him in the scene where he interacts with the bully, Jessie, who spits on him. For the first fifteen minutes in the film, Seth walks around with an aura that is filled to the brim with confidence, if not arrogance. When he encounters Jessie, however, he is completely at a loss for words. He never even attempts to stand up for himself, and within that one pivotal moment, the film lets you in on who Seth really is. Seth isn't a bully. His character is all talk, because that's all he really knows.

Casting Jonah Hill as Seth was a major boon for the character, as Hill has a surprisingly lovable charm that allows him to successfully make the average foulmouthed high school stereotype more relatable. As such, the character ages well. At the end of the day, Seth is just exemplifying how certain kids talk when no adults are around. Says Apatow, "I think Jonah was perfect because you always feel that he's a great guy underneath his bravado and his false confidence. You know what's going on, and you love him for trying. He's acting like he's very confident, but we know he's the least confident person in the world. He's a sweet, lonely guy who wishes somebody would love him."[2]

"Jonah came in looking like a deer in the headlights," Mottola says about seeing Hill read for Seth the first time. "And he said almost all of this stuff with a kind of panic and a terror in his eyes that makes you think *Oh, it's all bluster. He doesn't know the first thing about how to seduce a woman.* It's bluster mixed with hormones, and that's real. Jonah brought so much vulnerability to the character and so humanized him."[3]

That's not to say that there aren't those who disagree with this take. In the years that have followed, the film has been reassessed in light of how society has shifted. A popular podcast, *The Bechdel Cast*, examines how women are represented in film. They reviewed

172   I AM MCLOVIN

Superbad in 2017 and from minute one take issue with how the characters are portrayed. One of the hosts even says, "It's a bad movie for women. And I think in general history will forget it."[4]

In 2018, journalist Nina Metz published an exposé in the *Chicago Tribune* titled "How Teen Comedies like *Superbad* Normalize Sexual Assault." Obviously, there's a lot to unpack with that headline alone. While Metz does point to other comedies, *Superbad* is at the center of the piece.

Metz writes in the piece, "Evan (Cera) and Seth (Hill) are the movie's heroes—endearingly dorky, comically profane and obsessed with sex—and it is their close friendship and chatty comedic boorishness (whenever we see their point-of-view gaze in the direction of a woman or teenage girl, the camera zeroes in on her breasts) that gives the story shape and purpose." Metz continues, "But you can't escape that nasty premise, no matter how humorously it's dressed up—no matter how exuberantly it's passed off as teenage raunch. Of course the movie doesn't paint the boys as monsters. That's what makes this trope so effective—they're not the villains here. And here we butt up against the limits of comedy."[5]

The "nasty premise" she's referring to is the idea of buying alcohol for the object of one's affection in order to get them drunk enough that they'll acquiesce to sex. This is something Mottola views a bit differently.

Mottola says, "There's the irony obviously that Emma Stone's character doesn't drink, doesn't party. [Seth's] hoping that she'll loosen up and perhaps lower her standards to hook up with him if she's drunk. To boil it down to boys who want to get girls drunk to have sex with them I think is not exactly what the movie's about. I think it's about boys who provide booze that girls willingly drink so then everyone's inhibitions are lowered. And the fact is that they can't actually do it. Certainly Michael Cera's character can't do it when Becca's wasted.

They're both drunk and it's just not in him. He's not that person. He won't take advantage of a drunk person. Seth just realizes how wrongheaded he's been [the next day]."[6]

As Apatow sums up the film's conclusion, "By the end of the movie, they've learned something about the fact that they need to respect women and treat them well. And when you do that, you've got a much better chance at someone not wanting to run away from you."[7]

Still, the film also has its defenders. In 2019, journalist Aisha Harris wrote an article for the *New York Times* titled "*Superbad & Me*" in which she talks about her relationship with the film. She says she watched it when it first came out on DVD, and she immediately loved it. Later on, her outlook changed on it as she viewed it through a different lens, but she still comes to the film's defense as a whole. In the piece, she does explore both sides of that argument.[8]

"Every now and then I would return to the movie, and it would be (mostly) like old times," Harris wrote about how she's responded to the film following more recent viewings, given how much has changed within our culture since she first fell in love with it. "At some point I was troubled by the casual, unchecked homophobia peppered throughout the dialogue, an unfortunately all-too-common side effect of revisiting the things you loved in your more oblivious youth." She adds, "Yet *Superbad* was far from ruined for me. It's still fun, and what I probably appreciate the most now is the film's surprisingly progressive (for its time) view that taking sexual advantage of drunk women is really not O.K."[9]

Seth Rogen has been open about the fact that times have changed since they made *Superbad*. He has gone on to embrace this change, and has even expressed that he would not write dialogue using some of the more problematic language if he were making the film today.

"It's funny looking at some of the movies we made in the last ten years under the lens of new eras," Rogen later said in an interview. "Some new social consciousness. And yeah, there's for sure some stuff in our earlier movies—and even our more recent movies— where a year later you go, 'Eh, that maybe wasn't the greatest idea.' There are probably some jokes in *Superbad* that are bordering on blatantly homophobic at times. I mean, they're all in the voice of high school kids who do speak like that. But I think we'd also be silly not to acknowledge that we were also glamorizing that type of language in a lot of ways."[10]

For many, the rest of the film still holds up just as well as it ever did. Nothing in the film looks dated, either, which is due to the production team. Despite the fact that the film has a consistent '70s vibe throughout, you'll also notice a lack of overbearing technology in the film. All of the characters have flip phones, which makes sense when you figure that they shot it in 2006. But we also hardly see them using the technology. When they do, they don't get a great signal. But they don't go into withdrawals for not having better connection, like you may see a character do today. They just go about their day and focus on interacting with friends. This allows the film to remain modern but also have moments of nostalgia, so those in the audience who were in high school before cell phones can relate.

Social media has also kept *Superbad*'s status alive over the years with the nostalgia factor. So many millennials have a particular fondness for looking back and revering the things that they grew up with. One of those many things that people have a fondness for is *Superbad*. It's that nostalgia factor that has allowed the film to still thrive in this brand-new medium.

On TikTok, you will see tons of praise for the movie. From fans visiting the exact liquor store where McLovin got punched to Casey Margolis—who played young Seth in the movie—going viral by talking about his experience of making the film, *Superbad* remains in the public consciousness to this day. It's gotten to the point where even Generation Z has jumped on the *Superbad* bandwagon—these kids were barely even alive when *Superbad* came out. There's just something in it for everybody, and new fans keep on discovering it. It's an endless cycle.

Superbad was also an early entry into the bromance subgenre. A full year and a half before Jason Segel and Paul Rudd would help define the genre with *I Love You Man*, *Superbad* made no secret about the fact that it was about two men who shared strong, powerful connections. Sure, the film tricks you in the first two acts into thinking that the characters are drifting apart instead of coming together. But by the third act, it becomes clear that their friendship is the glue that has been holding this raucous comedy together the entire time. That's what defines a good bromance.

The bromance angle isn't the only avenue via which the film has found its way into the pop culture lexicon. The "I am McLovin" quote is also at the forefront of the film's place in pop culture. But a throwaway reference that Jonah Hill made during the soccer sequence has possibly even surpassed that.

DTF—which stands for "down to fuck"—was the name of a tagging crew of kids that he grew up with. When Hill says in the film "She's DTF. She's down to fuck," that was just something he threw in as a shout-out to his friends. He didn't think much of it, and it made its way into the movie. Then in late 2009, the reality show *Jersey Shore* also found itself among the pop culture landscape. One of the characters—Mike "The Situation" Sorrentino—adopted "DTF" as a catchphrase, lifting it from *Superbad*. It immediately started to take off. "[My tagging crew friends] were really pissed off," Hill recalled. "The Situation . . . made T-shirts and made a lot of money off it. I just thought it was so interesting—you say this thing that comes across your mind in a moment and then it's just there forever."[11]

For years Emma Stone would walk through malls or parking lots and be met with a barrage of people shouting at her and asking if she's "DTF." This happened pretty consistently. The same happened to Martha MacIsaac, who would have people shouting "I want a blowjay" at her. That's not exactly what you want people shouting at you in public, but unfortunately it kept happening.

Rogen doesn't have any problem embracing most of the film's legacy. He remains immensely proud of *Superbad*, and that is why he is so insistent to this day that there cannot be a sequel. If there's one aspect of *Superbad* that doesn't sit right with him in the years that have passed, it's been his interaction with certain members of law enforcement and how they feel about their portrayal in the film. You'd expect them to be pissed about seeing their profession caricatured in the film by a couple of incompetent badge abusers. But some officers have embraced those depictions, feeling a sense of pride about being associated with the film in such a way. Rogen isn't having it: "What's horrifying is a comment I get a lot where cops come up to me and say, 'I became a cop because of *Superbad*.' That has been said to me on numerous occasions. And when they say that to me, I say, 'That is fucked up. You did not understand the movie.'"[12]

Times may have changed in regards to what is acceptable in a post-#MeToo world, but one element of *Superbad* that ironically holds up the most is the depiction of the two police officers. At the time the film came out, you would have been forgiven for questioning whether or not actual cops like this even existed. Given what we've seen in the years since, not only has it become clear that are there cops on the job that are this irresponsible, but it's a way more common phenomenon than you might think.

What manages to hold its own in the ever-changing pop culture landscape seems completely random. Films like *Borat* and *The Hangover* were cash cows in theaters, but they got the added bump of being highly profitable from a merchandising aspect. The same could be said for *Superbad*. The McLovin ID is everywhere. Today, you're less likely to find a reference to *The Hangover*. But the McLovin ID still has its own spot at Target, and as long as Target continues to carry licensed T-shirts, McLovin will have a place to call home.

Afterword

There are few times in life when you manage to have all of the right cards in your hand. As audience members, we may not realize just how lucky it is to have all of the elements come together so perfectly in a film. Of course, talent plays a major part in anything you do that's creative, but it still has to coalesce. And that's what happened with *Superbad*, which has remained entrenched in our pop culture. It's not something that should be taken for granted—it's a gift.

Everybody who worked on the film knew just how special it was from the moment they first read the script. They may not have known how big the film would go on to become or that we'd still be talking about it all these years later, but they certainly knew how great it was at the time. The process of getting it made never felt so much like *if* but *when*. The filmmakers knew that as soon as someone would let them realize their vision on the big screen, they would find some sort of audience. It all comes back to timing.

"I've always believed there's a moment early in your career where you tell the story that means more than any other story," Apatow says of Rogen and Goldberg's commitment to making the film. "And when you can capture that, those become the timeless movies that people really remember. That's what *Superbad* was to Seth and Evan. It's just a very special moment where your passion level is through the roof to get a personal story out. And it definitely was a magical time where everybody was firing all on cylinders and working so hard at being so hilarious. Seth and Evan were just on fire, and Greg Mottola and the cast. It was like when you try to put together the perfect band, this was our supergroup."[1]

If that same supergroup tried to make *Superbad* again, they wouldn't get the same results. That's because—much like high school—*Superbad* represents a certain time in everyone's lives where they were finally being validated. While everyone involved may be a household name now, at the time they were all just a bunch of people in their late teens and early twenties that got together to make something they thought was special. The whole process flew under the radar, which is a luxury the cast and crew wouldn't get to experience ever again. If they tried to do a sequel now, all of that passion and authenticity would be relegated to secondary status.

The authenticity doesn't just stop at the characters in the film. Rogen has maintained a reputation for being brutally honest in everything he says and does. He isn't someone who's afraid to speak how he feels on certain subjects. Going back to whether or not they knew they had something special, most creatives would be inclined to downplay that question of "Did you know we'd still be talking about *Superbad* all these years later?" A lot of times, they will assure you that "You never know what will or won't work. I had no idea." Rogen is clearly not most creatives faking modesty just to save face. Twenty-five-year-old Seth Rogen always knew how big it would be once someone took a chance on it.

"The day we got greenlit," he later said when asked when he knew the movie would be a success. "I had full confidence that the movie was gonna do great. I knew if we could just get it going. That's what me, Judd, Seth, Greg, and Shauna always talked about. *If we could get this greenlit and do it the way we want, it's going to work.* I will say with confidence we one hundred percent took its success for granted. In the most literal sense of that sentence. I was not surprised. It is something that I look back on, and I marvel at my attitude."[2]

Rogen would later contend that he has a far different approach to his films being released now, describing himself as being grateful for the experiences. At the time, however, it was understandable that he would be so confident. *Knocked Up* was a huge success when it opened, as was *The 40 Year-Old Virgin* two years earlier. There was clearly an appetite for this type of comedy, and both audiences and Hollywood were picking up on it. So why the hell wouldn't a twenty-five-year-old who's already out there making a name for himself think his latest project would be any different? From *Freaks and Geeks* to *Knocked Up* to even *Donnie Darko* and *Da Ali G Show*, he hadn't seen any project he worked on yet be met with anything but praise from critics and audiences.

It's a movie that continues to stand the test of time. Adam Sandler has told Jonah Hill that Hill is his daughter's favorite comedian, all because of *Superbad*. McLovin has become a staple of hip-hop, with performers like Wiz Khalifa and Wale name-dropping the character. Marshall Mathers—best known as Eminem and who is actually name-dropped in *Superbad*—was such a big fan that he worked references of the film into two of his songs, "Ballin' Uncontrollably" and "Hello Good Morning." Better yet, Mathers's love for the film runs so deep that when he shot a cameo for *Funny People*, all he could talk about was how much he loved Hill and that he wanted to meet him. Hill wasn't on set that day, but Mathers insisted that Hill come to the set on his day off just so he could meet him. Hill wound up obliging this request.

If any year showed off just how relevant *Superbad* has remained, it would be 2023. That year alone, there were two high-profile projects that featured characters watching the film. First, *Năi Nai and Wài Pó* is an Oscar-nominated documentary short that follows the director's grandmothers, who act more like sisters than in-laws and spend every waking moment together. One of those waking moments we see is the two of them watching the scene in *Superbad* where Fogell shoots at the car.

Also in 2023, the much-talked-about film *Saltburn*, directed by Emerald Fennell, shows the characters watching the film at home. This is a slight anachronism, however, as the film takes place in the summer of 2007 and *Superbad* wasn't released on DVD until that winter. However, Fennell defends the decision by saying that someone in the family got a DVD screener. Regardless, what matters is that *Superbad* is the rare film that can maintain its place in pop culture long after the theater has cleared out.

Because of the film's universal factor, teenagers today can relate to it when they stream it just as much as anyone who saw it in a theater in 2007. It's evergreen, and it's the sort of film that so many people can take something different from, usually depending on where you're at in your life. To some, it's nostalgic. To others, it's just a really funny movie. So long as people have friends they are so dependent on they're afraid of one day losing, *Superbad* is going to find its way into everyone's heart one way or another.

It's also got a special place in the hearts of every single person who was on set for the film. Everybody that talks about making the film only remembers what a great experience it was. Hill can't help but use the word "fun" multiple times in interviews when he's trying to accurately depict what that experience was like for him. According to Goldberg, everyone involved remains close to this day, and they still see one another on a pretty regular basis. That's something that happens more with casts of television shows that run for multiple seasons, not so much a movie cast that only worked together for forty days.

For Mottola, he returned to New York when the film came out, and he couldn't even believe what had just happened. "I was back in New York with my wife, and we were like 'I can't fucking believe this. This is crazy.' It was exciting. I knew it was special. I haven't had a success like that again, so I knew to enjoy it. The timing was great. It was nice to be reaffirmed that our instincts were not off. All the key decisions that we made on the movie. It was really fun."[3]

When you think about who is the most recognizable, obviously Christopher Mintz-Plasse will come to mind. That's because you're still bound to come across the fake ID shirt pretty frequently. It never went out of print. Mintz-Plasse has now had people shouting "McLovin!" at him for half of his life. Everyone goes through phases of how they reconcile with something they are so closely identified with. While *Superbad* was a major moment for everyone else involved, Mintz-Plasse undoubtedly gets the brunt of it, given his character's place in pop culture.

His recognizable face is ripe for garnering that type of attention wherever he goes. It gets even worse when he gets carded. He later recalled, "Everyone thinks that they're the first one to think of like, 'Do you have the other ID?' Young me would've been so annoyed with all that. Because there was a really good four-year period where I had that screamed at me everywhere I went. And it was pretty draining. Especially as a twenty-year-old who is trying to figure out who the fuck I am. My brain is still developing and trying to figure out my career path."[4]

But he's made peace with the character, and what it means to people. He's embraced it for what it is and thinks it's cool when he spots people wearing the shirt. If he sees someone wearing it, he may walk up to them and say something to see how long it takes them to recognize him. Hader went through a similar experience once when picking his daughter up from school. He noticed one of her friends was wearing a McLovin shirt. He waited to see if they'd recognize him from the film. They never did, and he opted against bringing it up. Instead, he just enjoyed the moment.

"It was just such a ridiculously joyful experience for all of us," Robertson adds of the experience of getting *Superbad* made. "We didn't want to go home at 5 a.m. We wanted to stay up and hang out with our friends more. It was a real bonding experience. All of the people in the movie are really close. We're very close to each other.

And in a way I don't feel like any of us have aged much maturity wise."[5]

For Emma Stone, she has "the best memories of working on that movie." The experience sort of tainted her expectations for what would come next. This is due to being in such a laid-back environment where the ability to improvise was not only permitted but encouraged. "I thought that every movie was going to be like that," she later said. "I was like 'Oh, this is fun. You can just make it up as you go.' But every movie is not like that."[6]

As for Hill, the most remarkable part about *Superbad* is the circumstances under which they got to make it. He later said, "I made a movie with most of my best friends that were in it or around making it. It couldn't have been more fun. We were all making each other laugh. We all felt like we were on the right track at least. The whole reason the movie was made was because we hate teen comedies. They're not honest. You don't feel like you relate to the characters and the people in the movie. The goal at least was to try to make *Superbad* a movie that people would not call BS on. If I'm not that person, I at least know that person or knew that person growing up."[7]

Within the last handful of years, it's become increasingly popular to say, "You couldn't do that these days." There's a strange idea that everything prior to the mid-2010s was sort of the "wild west" where you could make a movie about anything at all without any repercussions. Obviously, that's not exactly true. There have always been boundaries and parameters. There is a little bit of truth to that sentiment, though not for why one might think.

The reason you couldn't make a movie like *Superbad* today has more to do with how the media landscape has shifted and less to do with the fear of being canceled. Yes, there are a few things in the film that don't hold up so well. But you're bound to find that in any form of artistic expression. Art is always supposed to reflect the times. *Superbad* was just that, while still managing to feel like a throwback to a bygone era. It had its cake and ate it, too.

It would be tough to make a movie like *Superbad* today because the way in which we consume films has undeniably changed. *Superbad* was fortunate enough to come along at just the right time to refresh the genre, instigating an absolute frenzy for R-rated comedies, which had been dormant for years. It was at a time when you could get away with doing more and more on TV than ever before thanks to shows on HBO and Comedy Central, so the time was right for the film world to follow suit.

By 2007, those raunchy comedies of the '70s and '80s had achieved cult classic status. Teenagers had grown up watching the films on cable long after they left theaters, developing an appreciation for them. Given the limited options of television at the time—back when even one hundred television channels seemed like a lot—the younger generation was willing to take more of a chance on older films. The reason why these younger generations make an exception for *Superbad* could be because they've heard so much about it from the millennial generation. But perhaps more importantly, the entire cast is even more relevant in pop culture than when it came out. So when they're scrolling and see a movie starring Jonah Hill, Michael Cera, Seth Rogen, and Emma Stone, they're eager to take a chance on it. Thus, a new fan is born.

Streaming has also affected theatrically released comedies because fewer people have been going out to the theater every year. As much as streaming has helped *Superbad*—and, let's be honest, a lot of movies—stay relevant, that doesn't mean it would allow such lighting to be caught in a bottle again. Unless your movie has a superhero in it, you're going to have a tougher time getting asses into seats. With even superhero movies becoming harder sells, you're going to see fewer studios taking chances on raunch comedies—in fact, comedies in general—as a result.

Take a movie like *Cocaine Bear*. When the trailer was released online in late 2022, it instantly went viral. The idea that Universal was putting out a movie about a bear that broke into a duffel bag full of cocaine surely was a fever dream of some sort. But it was very real, and there was a feeling around it that this film could break the curse that had plagued theatrically released comedies. This could be a return to a form that had been dormant for years.

Then the film was released in February 2023. Budgeted at $30–35 million, the film wound up bringing in $90 million domestically. Yes, it's a respectable number, as it basically tripled the initial investment. But for a film that was met with so much initial online interest, the studio was expecting more word-of-mouth attention than it ultimately wound up getting. Instead, it was in theaters for a month before making its way to Peacock. Momentum is hard to sustain now, no matter how badly it seems people want to see a film when the trailer is first dropped.

So no, you couldn't make *Superbad* in the same way under the exact circumstances. It was the perfect film for that moment in time, and it still manages to make us laugh all these years later.

"The part that I'm most proud of is that we all hung in there," Apatow recalls. "We all loved it so much that no matter what was happening in our lives or our careers, we had one eye on the ball to hopefully one day be allowed to get Superbad made."[8]

Years after the film came out, Rogen would reflect, "I think it's only in the last few years that I've grasped *We're like one of those high school movies that's stood the test of time*. You don't know that that's going to happen until years and years and years go by. Now that years and years and years have gone by, me and Evan look at each other and we're like, *We did it*."[8]

Acknowledgments

 ome projects resonate with you more than others. Movies resonate with us for different reasons. For me, with *Superbad*, it is
all connected to where I was in my life when I saw it. When I was
fourteen years old, I saw *Superbad* in theaters the Friday night that
it came out. All the buzz the film was getting convinced me that I
had to see it the first moment I possibly could. I vividly recall sitting
in my bedroom and reading articles that were—already—calling
it one of the greatest, raunchiest comedies of all time. So I went.
Because I was so young—and none of my friends could drive us to
the theater—I wound up seeing it with the next best thing: my dad
and my grandfather. It was something of a male bonding experience, and one of only two times I can count the three generations of
us guys getting together to do something like this. I've always had
a sense of pride that I caught on to the bloodstain joke about five
seconds before my dad did. He may dispute this, but I swear it's the
absolute truth.

To this day, that screening in a Lake Zurich, Illinois, Regal Cin-
emas remains the greatest screening of any film I've ever attended.
Of the thousands that I've been to by now—in art house theaters to
renovated movie palaces to premieres to run-down theaters in the
suburbs that feel practically forgotten to time—it remains the only
time I was actually concerned about the crowd's laughing causing
structural damage to the building. That is how wild it was. It was an
adrenaline rush that I've spent the rest of my life trying to find again

in a movie theater. So far, I've come up short. Something tells me it'll stay that way, too. Just like the conditions for making the film for those involved were special, so were the circumstances under which I saw it for the first time.

So when I first had the idea of giving *Superbad* the oral history treatment for *Vanity Fair* back in 2022, it was because I had a strong connection to the material. I knew I wanted to get everyone together to share their stories of just how this film came to be. When you do an oral history, there's always one or two holdouts. With *Superbad*, everybody I asked to participate said yes. That's how fondly everyone involved remembers the film to this day, and also how eager they all were to stroll down memory lane with me. For that oral history, I conducted interviews with Greg Mottola, Seth Rogen, Evan Goldberg, Judd Apatow, Jonah Hill, Michael Cera, Christopher Mintz-Plasse, Emma Stone, Bill Hader, Martha MacIsaac, and Shauna Robertson. The *Vanity Fair* interview I did with Rogen and Goldberg was so good that, even though schedule conflicts and the writers' and actors' strike didn't allow us to connect for the book, their presence can still be felt strongly throughout. Additionally, I have to thank Jeff Giles at *Vanity Fair* for letting me run with the idea and also putting up with my tendency to turn in pieces that are almost always way longer than he expects them to be. Sorry, Jeff!

Shortly after the oral history came out, my agent, Lee Sobel, approached me and presented me with the opportunity to turn it into a book. I didn't hesitate and leapt at it for two reasons. One: I had such a positive experience working on the oral history that it made me want to replicate that energy again, much like seeing the film for the first time. Like those who made the film, I wanted to catch lightning in a bottle again. More importantly, I knew that there was so much more to the story that my word count limitation at *Vanity Fair* wouldn't have allowed me to cover. I also wanted to have the chance to dedicate something to my dad and my late grandfather.

The journey to get to this point has been long, but also very rewarding. So much of the process for this book meant doing heavy amounts of research and trying to piece everything together. Luckily, *Superbad* was given such a royal treatment when it came out and was talked about by everyone, with the film's creatives doing press everywhere they could to get the word out, that I had reams of material at my fingertips when I was writing this book. From seventeen-year-old articles to blurry YouTube clips of the cast on the press circuit, I was able to obtain everything I needed and beyond to tell this story. It was like traveling down rabbit hole after rabbit hole, and the research delivered every single time I went down one.

I wasn't working on this book alone, though. First, I have to thank all the amazing participants who were nice enough to make themselves available for interviews. The film's director, Greg Mottola, proved to be a massive part of the process of writing this book. Despite his busy schedule, he participated in multiple interviews and fielded a multitude of questions as I tried to piece it all together. He was also kind enough to write the foreword for this book, and I cannot thank him enough for that. Similarly, Judd Apatow also managed to go out of his way over the years to assist with interviews on multiple projects I've worked on, including this one. As always, I'm looking forward to the next interview, Judd. This book would not be what it is without either of these two men, and I thank them for their time.

I also managed to round up an amazing lineup of participants who hadn't participated in the *Vanity Fair* oral history. This includes then–Sony Pictures president Amy Pascal, then–Columbia Pictures president Matt Tolmach, cinematographer Russ Alsobrook, production designer Chris Spellman, actress Aviva Baumann, music supervisor Jonathan Karp, and composer Lyle Workman. Every single person had great memories that added so much to the book, and all are responsible for helping to bring this to life.

I am also grateful to John Cerullo, Chris Chappell, and the team at Applause Books for giving this book a home. I also want to thank my agent, Lee Sobel, for getting this book sold and for being supportive of it from the beginning. These individuals all understood what the story of *Superbad* represents, and why it was so important for there to be a book on it.

Additionally, when you work on a book, it's impossible to take everything upon your own shoulders. It's crucial to surround yourself with colleagues and friends who can assist and champion the project along the way. As a result, this book would never have been possible without the following people who were always there with kindness, knowledge, and expertise, and who acted as a sounding board when I'd find myself occasionally unraveling: Cam Hines, Alan Siegel, Jeff Abraham, Michael Roffman, Stephen Frost, Richard Burgauer, Max Raimi, Tyler Kaufman, Michelle Barranco, Lauren Konze, Dexter Tardy, Abigail McGuire, Kim Goff, and Jada McWilliams, among countless others. I've always been a firm believer that my projects would be nothing without the people around me. So for that, I am forever indebted to all of you, and I had to make sure you all got your shout-outs for having my back.

Finally, this book is nothing without my ever-patient family, who have all been so supportive of my career as a whole, showing up to every play I was in as an actor growing up, my stand-up shows as a teenager, and my book signings as an adult. This includes my grandparents Sylvia, John, Joanne, and Don; my cousins Ariana, Tara, Kyle, Kari, Carys, Michael, Amanda, Dani, Walt, Graham, and Kris; and my countless aunts and uncles, Greg, Sue, Lee, Don, Stephanie, John, Laura, Dan, Michelle, and Deb. Of course, I have to especially shout out my parents, Ron and Juli Buss, and my sister, Becca. I cannot thank them enough for watching me struggle for years writing for free and giving me the room I needed to find my own way. Their support is what has kept me thriving for all these years. Dad, I have to thank you and Papa—Don Buss—for indulging your comedy-obsessed teenager and bringing him to see *Superbad.* You clearly had no idea what you were getting yourself into with that one. But I'm forever grateful that you never came to your senses.

Notes

Chapter 1

1. Seth Rogen and Sam Jones, interview (https://www.youtube.com/watch?v=G2ZzBmMRH7I).

2. *Superbad* commentary.

3. Seth Rogen and Evan Goldberg, interview with the author for *Vanity Fair*, 2022.

4. Seth Rogen and Judd Apatow at the 2007 *New Yorker* Festival (https://www.youtube.com/watch?v=BB80Fm4pwgo&t=126s).

5. Seth Rogen and Evan Goldberg, "From Script to Screen" (https://scriptmag.com/features/seth-rogen-evan-goldberg-super-bad-script-to-screen).

6. Seth Rogen and Evan Goldberg, interview with the author for *Vanity Fair*, 2022.

7. Seth Rogen and Evan Goldberg, interview with the author for *Vanity Fair*, 2022.

8. Seth Rogen, early stand-up (https://www.youtube.com/watch?v=jxlQgFTcfNs).

9. Seth Rogen, early stand-up (https://www.youtube.com/watch?v=jxlQgFTcfNs).

10. *Superbad* commentary.

11. Seth Rogen and Evan Goldberg, interview with the author for *Vanity Fair*, 2022.

12. Sammy Fogell interview (https://www.cbc.ca/news/canada/british-columbia/seth-rogen-s-vancouver-high-school-misadventures-hit-the-big-screen-1.668110).

13. Seth Rogen interview (https://movieweb.com/seth-rogen -evan-goldberg-greg-mottola-and-judd-apatow-make-a-film-that-is -superbad/).

14. Seth Rogen interview (https://movieweb.com/seth-rogen -evan-goldberg-greg-mottola-and-judd-apatow-make-a-film-that-is -superbad/).

Chapter 2

1. Judd Apatow, *New Yorker* interview (https://www.newyorker.com/ culture/the-new-yorker-interview/judd-apatow-is-still-an-optimist).

2. Judd Apatow, Steve Martin photoshoot (https://www.vanityfair .com/video/watch/steve-martin-and-judd-apatow-discuss-their-first -encounter).

3. Judd Apatow, Steve Martin photoshoot (https://www.vanityfair .com/video/watch/steve-martin-and-judd-apatow-discuss-their-first -encounter).

4. *Vanity Fair, Freaks and Geeks* oral history (https://www.vanityfair .com/hollywood/2013/01/freaks-and-geeks-oral-history).

5. Judd Apatow, *The Howard Stern Show*, 2015 (https://www.youtube .com/watch?v=gnQuNRdlMsw).

6. *Washington Post, Freaks and Geeks* oral history (https://www.wash ingtonpost.com/arts-entertainment/2021/01/27/freaks-and-geeks-stream ing-hulu-cast-creators-interview/).

7. *Washington Post, Freaks and Geeks* oral history (https://www.wash ingtonpost.com/arts-entertainment/2021/01/27/freaks-and-geeks-stream ing-hulu-cast-creators-interview/).

8. *Vanity Fair, Freaks and Geeks* oral history (https://www.vanityfair .com/hollywood/2013/01/freaks-and-geeks-oral-history).

9. *Hollywood Reporter, Freaks and Geeks* review (https://www.holly woodreporter.com/news/general-news/freaks-geeks-first-episodes-1999 -816674).

10. Seth Rogen, *GQ* interview (https://www.gq.com/story/seth-rogen -pineapple-express).

11. The Ringer, *Superbad* article (https://www.theringer.com/pop-culture/2017/8/30/16222874/superbad-ten-years-later-seth-rogen-judd-apatow).

12. JoBlo, *Freaks and Geeks* article (https://www.joblo.com/freaks-and-geeks-judd-apatow-season-2-mtv/).

13. NME, *Freaks and Geeks* season 2 (https://www.nme.com/features/tv-features/freaks-and-geeks-season-2-1969369).

14. Seth Rogen, early interview (https://www.youtube.com/watch?v=DcJGrUa56ec).

15. Garth Ancier, *Freaks and Geeks* criticism (https://www.tvguide.com/news/freaks-geeks-seth-rogen-cancellation-nbc-garth-ancier-1088062/).

16. Seth Rogen, *GQ* interview (https://www.gq.com/story/seth-rogen-pineapple-express).

17. Judd Apatow, interview with the author for *Vanity Fair*, 2022.

18. Seth Rogen, *EW* interview (https://ew.com/article/2007/08/15/superbad-raucous-roundtable-part-3/).

19. The Ringer, *Superbad* article (https://www.theringer.com/pop-culture/2017/8/30/16222874/superbad-ten-years-later-seth-rogen-judd-apatow).

20. Seth Rogen, Collider interview (https://collider.com/seth-rogen-interview-knocked-up/).

21. Judd Apatow, *Time* interview (https://web.archive.org/web/20070519210644/http://www.time.com/time/magazine/article/0,9171,1622581,00.html).

22. *New York Post*, *Undeclared* article (https://nypost.com/2002/01/13/unexplainedabsences/).

Chapter 3

1. Greg Mottola, interview with the author for *Vanity Fair*, 2022.

2. Greg Mottola, interview with the author for *Vanity Fair*, 2022.

3. Seth Rogen and Judd Apatow at the 2007 *New Yorker* Festival (https://www.youtube.com/watch?v=BB80Fm4pwgo&t=126s).

4. *Yearbook* by Seth Rogen.

5. *Yearbook* by Seth Rogen.

6. Judd Apatow, interview with the author for *Vanity Fair*, 2022.

7. The Ringer, *Superbad* article (https://www.theringer.com/pop-culture/2017/8/30/16222874/superbad-ten-years-later-seth-rogen-judd-apatow).

8. The Ringer, *Superbad* article (https://www.theringer.com/pop-culture/2017/8/30/16222874/superbad-ten-years-later-seth-rogen-judd-apatow).

9. Seth Rogen, *EW* Interview (https://ew.com/article/2007/08/15/superbad-raucous-roundtable-part-3/).

10. Seth Rogen and Evan Goldberg, "From Script to Screen" (https://scriptmag.com/features/seth-rogen-evan-goldberg-super-bad-script-to-screen).

11. Seth Rogen and Evan Goldberg, "From Script to Screen" (https://scriptmag.com/features/seth-rogen-evan-goldberg-super-bad-script-to-screen).

12. Seth Rogen, 10th anniversary tweet (https://www.complex.com/pop-culture/a/tracewilliamcowen/seth-rogen-superbad-trivia-10th-anniversary).

13. Seth Rogen and Evan Goldberg, "From Script to Screen" (https://scriptmag.com/features/seth-rogen-evan-goldberg-super-bad-script-to-screen).

14. The Ringer, *Superbad* article (https://www.theringer.com/pop-culture/2017/8/30/16222874/superbad-ten-years-later-seth-rogen-judd-apatow).

15. Judd Apatow, interview with the author, 2024.

16. Seth Rogen and Evan Goldberg, interview with the author for *Vanity Fair*, 2022.

17. Seth Rogen and Evan Goldberg, interview with the author for *Vanity Fair*, 2022.

18. Seth Rogen, *OC Register* interview (https://www.ocregister.com/2007/08/16/fast-times-for-superbad-creator-seth-rogen/).

19. Seth Rogen, *GQ* interview (https://www.gq.com/story/seth-rogen-pineapple-express).

20. Seth Rogen, *GQ* interview (https://www.gq.com/story/seth-rogen -pineapple-express).

21. Seth Rogen and Judd Apatow at the 2007 *New Yorker* Festival (https://www.youtube.com/watch?v=BB80Fm4pwgo&t=126s).

22. Seth Rogen and Judd Apatow at the 2007 *New Yorker* Festival (https://www.youtube.com/watch?v=BB80Fm4pwgo&t=126s).

23. Seth Rogen and Judd Apatow at the 2007 *New Yorker* Festival (https://www.youtube.com/watch?v=BB80Fm4pwgo&t=126s).

Chapter 4

1. Judd Apatow, *New York Times* profile (https://www.nytimes.com /2007/05/27/magazine/27apatow-t.html).

2. Seth Rogen and Judd Apatow at the 2007 *New Yorker* Festival (https://www.youtube.com/watch?v=BB80Fm4pwgo&t=126s).

3. Seth Rogen, *OC Register* interview (https://www.ocregister.com /2007/08/16/fast-times-for-superbad-creator-seth-rogen/).

4. Seth Rogen and Evan Goldberg, "From Script to Screen" (https:// scriptmag.com/features/seth-rogen-evan-goldberg-super-bad-script-to -screen).

5. Seth Rogen and Evan Goldberg, interview with the author for *Vanity Fair*, 2022.

6. Amy Pascal, interview with the author, 2024.

7. Matt Tolmach, interview with the author, 2024.

8. Matt Tolmach, interview with the author, 2024.

9. Judd Apatow, interview with the author, 2024.

10. Amy Pascal, interview with the author, 2024.

Chapter 5

1. Matt Tolmach, interview with the author, 2024.

2. Greg Mottola, interview with the author, 2024.

3. Greg Mottola, interview with the author for *Vanity Fair*, 2022.

4. Judd Apatow, IGN interview (https://www.ign.com/articles/2007/07/09/set-visit-superbad).

5. Shauna Robertson, interview with the author for *Vanity Fair*, 2022.

6. Seth Rogen and Evan Goldberg, interview with the author for *Vanity Fair*, 2022.

7. Seth Rogen and Evan Goldberg, interview with the author for *Vanity Fair*, 2022.

8. Michael Cera, interview with the author for *Vanity Fair*, 2022.

9. Michael Cera, *Superbad* audition tape.

10. Michael Cera, *Far Out Magazine* article (https://faroutmagazine.co.uk/michael-cera-cast-the-sixth-sense/).

11. Judd Apatow interview with the author for *Vanity Fair*, 2022.

12. Seth Rogen and Evan Goldberg interview with the author for *Vanity Fair*, 2022.

13. Seth Rogen and Jonah Hill, Backstage interview (https://www.backstage.com/magazine/article/jonah-hill-seth-rogen-interview-superbad-35172/).

14. Greg Mottola, interview with the author for *Vanity Fair*, 2022.

15. Jonah Hill, Michael Cera, and Christopher Mintz-Plasse, Movieweb interview (https://movieweb.com/jonah-hill-michael-cera-and-christopher-mintz-plasse-are-superbad).

16. *Superbad* commentary.

17. Judd Apatow, interview with the author for *Vanity Fair*, 2022.

18. Jonah Hill, *Superbad* audition tape.

19. Seth Rogen and Evan Goldberg, interview with the author for *Vanity Fair*, 2022.

20. Jonah Hill, Michael Cera, Christopher Mintz-Plasse, Groucho Reviews interview (https://www.grouchoreviews.com/interviews/6334f8475fe75d1811c62733).

21. Matt Tolmach, interview with the author, 2024.

22. Michael Cera and Christopher Mintz-Plasse, *Superbad* interview (https://collider.com/michael-cera-and-christopher-mintzplasse-interview-superbad/).

23. Jonah Hill, Michael Cera, and Christopher Mintz-Plasse, Movieweb interview (https://movieweb.com/jonah-hill-michael-cera-and -christopher-mintz-plasse-are-superbad).

24. Greg Mottola, interview with the author for *Vanity Fair*, 2022.

25. Judd Apatow, interview with the author for *Vanity Fair*, 2022.

26. Greg Mottola, interview with the author for *Vanity Fair*, 2022.

27. Amy Pascal, interview with the author, 2024.

28. *Superbad* oral history (https://www.vanityfair.com/hollywood/2022 /08/superbad-oral-history?_sp=3db285e6-c1af-4737-a8aa-3c3d837a6c1f .1724466318639).

29. Matt Tolmach, interview with the author, 2024.

30. *Superbad* Watch Party Cast Reunion (https://www.youtube.com/ watch?v=UcdIwLGDsiU).

31. Judd Apatow, interview with the author for *Vanity Fair*, 2022.

32. Aviva Baumann, interview with the author, 2024.

33. Seth Rogen and Evan Goldberg, interview with the author for *Vanity Fair*, 2022.

34. Judd Apatow, interview with the author for *Vanity Fair*, 2022.

35. Bill Hader, interview with the author for *Vanity Fair*, 2022.

Chapter 6

1. Matt Tolmach, interview with the author, 2024.

2. Seth Rogen and Evan Goldberg, interview with the author for *Vanity Fair*, 2022.

3. Judd Apatow, *New York Times* profile (https://www.nytimes.com /2007/05/27/magazine/27apatow-t.html).

4. Allison Jones, *Hollywood Reporter* interview (https://www.holly woodreporter.com/tv/tv-news/freaks-geeks-a-simple-favor-paul-feigs -secret-weapon-1141139/).

5. Christopher Mintz-Plasse, KTLA interview (https://www.youtube .com/watch?v=SNeEGXqxK6s).

6. Christopher Mintz-Plasse, interview with the author for *Vanity Fair*, 2022.

7. Allison Jones, *New Yorker* interview (https://www.newyorker.com/magazine/2015/04/06/the-nerd-hunter).

8. Christopher Mintz-Plasse, *Superbad* audition tape.

9. Greg Mottola, interview with the author for *Vanity Fair*, 2022.

10. Christopher Mintz-Plasse, *Superbad* audition tape.

11. Judd Apatow, interview with the author for *Vanity Fair*, 2022.

12. Christopher Mintz-Plasse, interview with the author for *Vanity Fair*, 2022.

13. Christopher Mintz-Plasse, CinemaBlend interview (https://www.cinemablend.com/interviews/superbads-christopher-mintz-plasse-sets-the-record-straight-on-beef-with-jonah-hill).

14. Judd Apatow, interview with the author for *Vanity Fair*, 2022.

15. Greg Mottola, interview with the author, 2024.

Chapter 7

1. Greg Mottola, interview with the author for *Vanity Fair*, 2022.

2. Seth Rogen and Judd Apatow, at the 2007 *New Yorker* Festival (https://www.youtube.com/watch?v=BB80Fm4pwgo&t=126s).

3. Judd Apatow, interview with the author, 2024.

4. Russ T. Alsobrook, interview with the author, 2024.

5. Greg Mottola, interview with the author for *Vanity Fair*, 2022.

6. Chris Spellman, interview with the author, 2024.

7. *Superbad* Watch Party Cast Reunion (https://www.youtube.com/watch?v=UcdIwLGDsiU).

8. Chris Spellman, interview with the author, 2024.

9. Debra McGuire, *Interview Magazine* article (https://www.interviewmagazine.com/fashion/superbad-costume-designer-talks-working-emma-stone-first-major-role).

10. Jonah Hill, Michael Cera, and Christopher Mintz-Plasse, Movieweb interview (https://movieweb.com/jonah-hill-michael-cera-and-christopher-mintz-plasse-are-superbad).

11. Seth Rogen and Jonah Hill, Backstage interview (https://www .backstage.com/magazine/article/jonah-hill-seth-rogen-interview-super bad-35172/).

12. Judd Apatow, interview with the author, 2024.

13. Jonah Hill, Ain't It Cool interview (https://legacy.aintitcool.com/ node/32784).

Chapter 8

1. *Superbad* soccer field scene.

2. Judd Apatow, interview with the author, 2024.

3. *Superbad* DVD featurette.

4. *Superbad* DVD featurette.

5. Greg Mottola, interview with the author, 2024.

6. *Superbad* convenience store scene.

7. *Superbad* DVD featurette.

8. Shauna Robertson, interview with the author for *Vanity Fair*, 2022.

9. Matt Tolmach, interview with the author, 2024.

10. *Superbad* Watch Party Cast Reunion (https://www.youtube.com/ watch?v=UcdIwLGDsiU).

11. Seth Rogen on *Life Is Short* podcast with Justin Long.

12. Jonah Hill, Black Film interview (https://www.blackfilm.com /20070810/features/superbadcast.shtml).

13. *Superbad* E! cast interviews (https://www.youtube.com/watch?v =gK5YZedVITY&t=107s).

14. Jonah Hill. Black Film interview (https://www.blackfilm.com /20070810/features/superbadcast.shtml).

15. Seth Rogen and Jonah Hill, Backstage interview (https://www .backstage.com/magazine/article/jonah-hill-seth-rogen-interview-super bad-35172/).

16. Seth Rogen and Evan Goldberg, interview with the author for *Vanity Fair*, 2022.

17. Seth Rogen and Evan Goldberg, interview with the author for *Vanity Fair*, 2022.

18. Bill Hader, interview with the author for *Vanity Fair*, 2022.

19. *Superbad* E! cast interviews (https://www.youtube.com/watch?v=gK5YZedVITY&t=107s).

20. Greg Mottola, interview with the author, 2024.

21. *Superbad* Watch Party Cast Reunion (https://www.youtube.com/watch?v=UcdIwLGDsiU).

22. Michael Cera, *Esquire* interview (https://www.youtube.com/watch?v=OXdexPhsNHg).

23. Aviva Baumann, interview with the author, 2024.

24. Greg Mottola, interview with the author, 2024.

25. Shauna Robertson, interview with the author for *Vanity Fair*, 2022.

26. Greg Mottola, MovieWeb interview (https://movieweb.com/seth-rogen-evan-goldberg-greg-mottola-and-judd-apatow-make-a-film-that-is-superbad/).

27. Michael Cera, interview with the author for *Vanity Fair*, 2022.

28. Bill Hader, interview with the author for *Vanity Fair*, 2022.

29. Christopher Mintz-Plasse, interview with the author for *Vanity Fair*, 2022.

30. Bill Hader, interview with the author for *Vanity Fair*, 2022.

31. Christopher Mintz-Plasse, interview with the author for *Vanity Fair*, 2022.

32. Bill Hader, interview with the author for *Vanity Fair*, 2022.

33. Greg Mottola, interview with the author, 2024.

34. Seth Rogen and Evan Goldberg, "From Script to Screen" (https://scriptmag.com/features/seth-rogen-evan-goldberg-super-bad-script-to-screen).

35. Judd Apatow, interview with the author for *Vanity Fair*, 2022.

36. Shauna Robertson, interview with the author for *Vanity Fair*, 2022.

Chapter 9

1. Greg Mottola, interview with the author for *Vanity Fair*, 2022.

2. Judd Apatow, interview with the author for *Vanity Fair*, 2022.

3. Greg Mottola, interview with the author, 2024.

4. Seth Rogen and Evan Goldberg, interview with the author for *Vanity Fair*, 2022.

5. Matt Tolmach, interview with the author, 2024.

6. Casey Margolis, TikTok (https://www.tiktok.com/@caseymargo lis_/video/7049937259109305647).

7. Laura Marano, Collider interview (https://collider.com/robert-de -niro-the-good-shepherd-sequel-war-with-grandpa-interview).

8. Christopher Mintz-Plasse, interview with the author for *Vanity Fair*, 2022.

9. Greg Mottola, interview with the author for *Vanity Fair*, 2022.

10. Christopher Mintz-Plasse, interview with the author for *Vanity Fair*, 2022.

11. Aviva Baumann, interview with the author, 2024.

12. *Superbad* Watch Party Cast Reunion (https://www.youtube.com/ watch?v=UcdIwLGDsiU).

13. *Superbad* Watch Party Cast Reunion (https://www.youtube.com/ watch?v=UcdIwLGDsiU).

14. *Superbad* Watch Party Cast Reunion (https://www.youtube.com/ watch?v=UcdIwLGDsiU).

15. *Superbad* Watch Party Cast Reunion (https://www.youtube.com/ watch?v=UcdIwLGDsiU).

16. *Superbad* Watch Party Cast Reunion (https://www.youtube.com/ watch?v=UcdIwLGDsiU).

Chapter 10

1. Greg Mottola, interview with the author, 2024.

2. Greg Mottola, interview with the author, 2024.

3. Greg Mottola, Movieweb interview (https://movieweb.com/seth -rogen-evan-goldberg-greg-mottola-and-judd-apatow-make-a-film-that -is-superbad/).

4. Greg Mottola, interview with the author, 2024.

5. Greg Mottola, interview with the author, 2024.

6. Michael Cera, *Hot Ones* (https://www.youtube.com/watch?v=uBJq-XCP27c).

7. Greg Mottola, interview with the author for *Vanity Fair*, 2022.

8. Greg Mottola, interview with the author for *Vanity Fair*, 2022.

9. Lyle Workman, interview with the author, 2024.

10. Jonathan Karp, interview with the author, 2024.

11. *Superbad* music recording featurette.

12. Lyle Workman interview with the author, 2024.

13. Judd Apatow, *EW Superbad* interviews (https://ew.com/article/2007/08/10/superbad-ews-raucous-roundtable-part-1/).

14. Seth Rogen, *EW Superbad* interviews (https://ew.com/article/2007/08/10/superbad-ews-raucous-roundtable-part-1/).

15. Greg Mottola, interview with the author, 2024.

16. Judd Apatow, interview with the author for *Vanity Fair*, 2022.

17. Greg Mottola, interview with the author for *Vanity Fair*, 2022.

18. Judd Apatow, interview with the author for *Vanity Fair*, 2022.

19. Greg Mottola, interview with the author, 2024.

20. Greg Mottola, interview with the author, 2024.

21. Matt Tolmach, interview with the author, 2024.

22. Judd Apatow, interview with the author, 2024.

23. Greg Mottola, interview with the author, 2024.

24. *Superbad EW* article (https://ew.com/article/2007/08/10/will-superbad-be-hit/).

25. Judd Apatow, interview with the author, 2024.

Chapter 11

1. Seth Rogen, *EW* interview (https://ew.com/article/2007/04/20/talking-seth-rogen/).

2. *Knocked Up*, Rotten Tomatoes (https://www.rottentomatoes.com/m/knocked_up).

3. Judd Apatow, Movieweb interview (https://movieweb.com/seth-rogen-evan-goldberg-greg-mottola-and-judd-apatow-make-a-film-that-is-superbad/).

4. Judd Apatow, *LA Times* interviews (https://www.latimes.com/archives/la-xpm-2008-mar-25-et-goldstein25-story.html).

5. *Superbad* premiere article, *LA Times* (https://www.latimes.com/entertainment/movies/la-et-sceniac14aug14-story.html).

6. *Superbad* premiere article, *LA Times* (https://www.latimes.com/entertainment/movies/la-et-sceniac14aug14-story.html).

7. Roger Ebert, *Superbad* review (https://www.rogerebert.com/reviews/superbad-2007).

8. *Superbad* review, *New York Magazine* (https://nymag.com/movies/reviews/36069).

9. *Superbad* review, *Newsweek* (https://www.newsweek.com/review-superbad-super-close-perfect-99083).

10. Matt Tolmach, interview with the author, 2024.

11. Seth Rogen and Evan Goldberg, interview with the author for *Vanity Fair*, 2022.

12. Seth Rogen and Evan Goldberg, interview with the author for *Vanity Fair*, 2022.

13. Aviva Baumann, interview with the author, 2024.

14. Jonah Hill, Oklahoman interview (https://www.oklahoman.com/story/news/2007/08/21/how-did-superbad-top-the-box-office/61732506007).

15. Greg Mottola, interview with the author, 2024.

16. Judd Apatow, interview with the author for *Vanity Fair*, 2022.

17. Jonah Hill, Huffington Post interview (https://www.huffpost.com/entry/jonah-hill-on-how-superbad-gay_n_972078).

18. Christopher Mintz-Plasse, interview with the author for *Vanity Fair*, 2022.

19. Michael Cera, *The Guardian* interview (https://www.theguardian.com/lifeandstyle/2023/jul/17/fame-makes-you-paranoid-michael-cera-on-barbie-drunk-fans-and-not-owning-a-smartphone).

20. Jonah Hill, *The Columbus Dispatch* profile (https://www.dispatch.com/story/entertainment/2012/07/24/profile-jonah-hill-stardom-odd/23587734007/).

21. Bill Hader, interview with the author for *Vanity Fair*, 2022.

22. Judd Apatow, interview with the author, 2024.

23. *Superbad* Watch Party Cast Reunion (https://www.youtube.com/watch?v=UcdIwLGDsiU).

24. Michael Cera, interview with the author for *Vanity Fair*, 2022.

25. Matt Tolmach, interview with the author, 2024.

26. Bill Hader, interview with the author for *Vanity Fair*, 2022.

27. Jonah Hill and Michael Cera, *The A24 Podcast* (https://a24films.com/notes/2019/01/dont-be-a-stranger-with-jonah-hill-and-michael-cera-1).

28. Christopher Mintz-Plasse, interview with the author for *Vanity Fair*, 2022.

29. Aviva Baumann, interview with the author, 2024.

30. Jonah Hill and Michael Cera, *The A24 Podcast* (https://a24films.com/notes/2019/01/dont-be-a-stranger-with-jonah-hill-and-michael-cera-1).

31. *Superbad EW* article (https://ew.com/article/2007/08/10/will-superbad-be-hit/).

32. Edgar Wright, *Superbad* junket interview (https://www.youtube.com/watch?v=OOjNQ57-pKQ).

33. Judd Apatow, interview with the author for *Vanity Fair*, 2022.

34. Judd Apatow, interview with the author for *Vanity Fair*, 2022.

35. Matt Tolmach, interview with the author, 2024.

36. Jonah Hill and Michael Cera, *The A24 Podcast* (https://a24films.com/notes/2019/01/dont-be-a-stranger-with-jonah-hill-and-michael-cera-1)

Chapter 12

1. Greg Mottola, interview with the author, 2024.

2. *Superbad* deleted scene.

3. Michael Cera, *Esquire* interview (https://www.youtube.com/watch?v=OXdexPhsNHg)

4. *Superbad* commentary.

5. Seth Rogen, *The Howard Stern Show* (https://www.youtube.com/watch?v=OnD6_-oVLEg).

6. Judd Apatow, Backstage interview (https://www.backstage.com/magazine/article/comedy-hard-judd-apatow-interview-17992/).

7. Michael Cera, *The Guardian* interview (https://www.theguardian.com/lifeandstyle/2023/jul/17/fame-makes-you-paranoid-michael-cera-on-barbie-drunk-fans-and-not-owning-a-smartphone).

8. Greg Mottola, interview with the author, 2024.

9. Seth Rogen and Evan Goldberg, interview with the author for *Vanity Fair*, 2022.

10. Indiewire *Superbad* sequel article (https://www.indiewire.com/features/general/superbad-2-judd-apatow-jonah-hill-sequel-plot-1234723799/).

11. *Superbad* commentary.

Chapter 13

1. Greg Mottola, interview with the author, 2024.

2. Judd Apatow, interview with the author, 2024.

3. Greg Mottola, interview with the author, 2024.

4. *The Bechdel Cast*, 2017 Patreon episode (https://www.patreon.com/posts/superbad-15355591).

5. Nina Metz, *Chicago Tribune* op-ed (https://www.chicagotribune.com/2018/10/03/how-teen-comedies-like-superbad-normalize-sexual-assault/).

6. Greg Mottola, interview with the author, 2024.

7. Judd Apatow, interview with the author, 2024.

8. *Superbad* op-ed, *New York Times* (https://www.nytimes.com/2019/08/05/arts/superbad-me.html).

9. *Superbad* op-ed, *New York Times* (https://www.nytimes.com/2019/08/05/arts/superbad-me.html).

10. Seth Rogen, *The Guardian* interview (https://www.theguardian.com/film/video/2016/may/04/seth-rogen-bad-neighbours-sorority-rising-chloe-grace-moretz-video-interview).

11. The Ringer, *Superbad* article (https://www.theringer.com/pop -culture/2017/8/30/16222874/superbad-ten-years-later-seth-rogen-judd -apatow).

12. Seth Rogen and Evan Goldberg, interview with the author for *Vanity Fair*, 2022.

Afterword

1.   Judd Apatow, interview with the author for *Vanity Fair*, 2022.

2.   Seth Rogen and Evan Goldberg, interview with the author for *Vanity Fair*, 2022.

3.   Greg Mottola, interview with the author for *Vanity Fair*, 2022.

4.   Christopher Mintz-Plasse, interview with the author for *Vanity Fair*, 2022.

5.   Shauna Robertson, interview with the author for *Vanity Fair*, 2022.

6.   Emma Stone, Interview Magazine (https://www.interviewmaga zine.com/film/emma-stone).

7.   *Superbad* E! cast interviews (https://www.youtube.com/watch?v =gK5YZedVITY&t=107s).

8.   Judd Apatow, interview with the author for *Vanity Fair*, 2022.

Index

Photo insert images are indicated by *p1*, *p2*, *p3*, etc.